Imagine
YOURSELF WELL

Books by Frank DeMarco

Fiction

Babe in the Woods

Messenger: A Sequel to Lost Horizon

Nonfiction

A Place to Stand

Afterlife Conversations with Hemingway:
A Dialogue on His Life, His Work and the Myth

The Cosmic Internet: Explanations from the Other Side

The Sphere and the Hologram:
Explanations from the Other Side

Chasing Smallwood: Talking with the Other Side

Muddy Tracks: Exploring an Unsuspected Reality

Imagine YOURSELF WELL

A Practical Guide to
Using Visualization to Improve
Your Health and Your Life

FRANK DeMARCO

RAINBOW RIDGE
BOOKS

Cover and Interior design by Frame25 Productions
Cover Photo © Meranda19 c/o Shutterstock.com

Published by:
Rainbow Ridge Books, LLC
140 Rainbow Ridge Road
Faber, Virginia 22938
434-361-1723

If you are unable to order this book from your local
bookseller, you may order directly from the distributor.

Square One Publishers, Inc.
115 Herricks Road
Garden City Park, NY 11040
Phone: (516) 535-2010
Fax: (516) 535-2014
Toll-free: 877-900-BOOK

Visit the author at:
www.hologrambooks.com

Library of Congress Cataloging-in-Publication Data applied for.

ISBN 978-1-937907-29-7

10 9 8 7 6 5 4 3 2

Printed on acid-free paper in the United States

To all those among us quietly practicing their healing skills, helping where they can.

Contents

Introduction   ix

Part One: Thinking Differently   **1**

Chapter 1: I Knew What, but I Didn't Know How   3

Chapter 2: Four Assumptions   13

Part Two: Taking Charge   **23**

Chapter 3: From Helpless
Victim to Consulting Detective   25

Chapter 4: Reprogramming Your Robots   35

Chapter 5: Imagination as a
Tool of Perception and Cure   45

Part Three: Living Right   **53**

Chapter 6: Intuitive Knowing   55

Chapter 7: Practices   65

Part Four: What Can Be Done   **75**

Chapter 8: Dealing with Myself   77

Chapter 9: Dealing with Others   91

Chapter 10: You Can Do This!   101

Appendix 1: Excerpt from The Cosmic Internet   109

Introduction

In this book you will find simple techniques to improve your health. They are free, they have no side effects, and they cannot interfere with any medicines you may be taking. You can mix them with whatever form of medical care you prefer. You can do them with your doctor's blessing, or you can keep them to yourself.

You *can* use these techniques, no matter how serious your present condition. Are you in continual pain? Seriously injured? Enduring a chronic degenerative condition? Whatever, it doesn't matter. You *can* use these techniques.

The only catch is that you cannot benefit from these techniques while actively disbelieving in them. You don't have to *believe*, but you do need to *suspend disbelief,* or nothing can happen. You cannot be open to new possibilities and at the same time be closed to them. It is that simple. And is it so hard, suspending disbelief? If you try and you can't make the techniques work for you, what have you lost? A little time. But if you succeed, you have more to gain than you can presently guess.

Please note, I do not promise you perfect health, any more than I promise you a life without problems. I have my own health problems, and anyway it seems to me that life could be described as a series of problems to be faced. I don't think that's at all a bad thing. It isn't like we're victims—as you shall see.

Neither should you get the idea that the state of your health in any way indicates your level of spiritual development. It would be a more convenient world—and a better behaved one—if the people at the highest spiritual level automatically enjoyed the best health, while those at the bottom of the spiritual scale endured suffering and misery. *That* would encourage people to work on their spiritual life! But your level of spiritual growth and awareness has little or nothing to do with your state of health, and I don't think it is very hard to figure out why that is. We are all working on different things in these lives of ours, and suffering can be a very powerful aid to growth.

In other words, affliction isn't necessarily always a bad thing, any more than perfect health is necessarily always a good thing. So much depends upon what is going on *within* the person, and no one is capable of judging this from the outside. Nonetheless, there is no reason why you shouldn't acquire more effective tools to improve your health.

Does this book give you everything you need to maintain your health? Well, yes and no. If you come down with a serious disease, chances are you are going to the doctor, if not the hospital. If you have trouble with your teeth, sooner or later you are going to go to the dentist. And sooner or later you are going to die of something, if only old age. But does that mean it isn't worthwhile to live according to the principles I have named here?

What would it be worth to you, to live in less fear? What would it be worth to be in greater connection to more parts of yourself than you once recognized? What would it be worth to recognize that your health is less a reaction to outside stress than an expression of what you are and what your life is? What is it worth to know that you and your family and friends need not be helpless before accident, and disease, and injury? Most of all, what is it worth to you to learn how to grow into so much more that you can become? Read on, and find out.

A word about the organization of the material.

First comes *Thinking Differently,* because as you think, so you are. Part One gives you a sense of how I see the world, and how I came to see it that way, because society's present beliefs about health and the body affect us all, consciously or otherwise. For you to change your health, you must be able to envision new possibilities. To do that, you need a reason to change what you believe.

Part Two, *Taking Charge,* provides the framework and techniques you need to go from being a passive observer of your health to an active creator and shaper of patterns. And, as you will see, this is not restricted to questions of health. A change in attitude will reshape not just your health but your life.

Hence, Part Three, *Living Right,* broadens the application of framework and techniques, because your life is about more than health alone.

Part Four, *What Can Be Done,* offers my insights, suggestions, and guesses as to what's really going on with our health and with our lives. Above all, it offers you my encouragement, and wraps up the *how* of imagining yourself well. It is true, what I promise: You can do this.

Part One

THINKING
DIFFERENTLY

Chapter 1

I Knew *What,* but I Didn't Know *How*

I got asthma, or *asthma* got *me,* when I was two years old, and we've lived together ever since. Some of my earliest memories involve doctors offices and trips to the hospital, and endless nights spent sitting on the side of the bed, fighting for the next breath. Anything could bring it on: intense emotion, too much running around, a change of season, even too much laughing. Anything. Sometimes, seemingly, nothing.

This was a long time ago—I was born in 1946—and inhalers were a thing of the future. Our doctor's arsenal amounted mostly to injections and pills. For years, I walked to the doctor's office after school twice a week for a shot of whatever it was. But even then, *something* within me *knew* that doctors and pills and shots weren't necessary. All that was needed was to—somehow—*turn* my mind a certain way and health would be there. If I could just remember how to do it, I could have miracles. I didn't know how I knew it, and I didn't know how to do it, but I knew it as well as I knew anything in my life, despite my day by day experience to the contrary.

I'd better say right here that what that boy knew wasn't wrong, but was incomplete. You *can* turn your mind a certain way, so to speak. Working from the "mind" end of the mind-body connection *will* give you a lot more control than you have now. That's what this little book is about. But the boy wasn't quite right, either, because he neglected to work from the "body" end of the connection.

I got my first glimpse into the mind-body connection in action a few weeks before I turned 21. I came home after my sophomore year in college, but before I could find a summer job—immediately, in fact—I fell into an asthma attack. It began Friday and continued, day and night, all weekend. Monday morning, June 5, 1967, I walked bleary-eyed into the kitchen and heard on the radio that the Six Day War had started. I had been half expecting it, but it was a shock nonetheless.

Evidently a shock was exactly what was needed. Before the broadcast ended, my lungs were functioning normally again, which they continued to do all summer.

For a long time this remained merely a puzzling incident. Three decades later, I read Dion Fortune's novel *The Sea Priestess*, and saw that the narrator, a middle-aged man with asthma, said that he had once fallen downstairs in the middle of an asthma attack and the shock had cured it instantly. So, the phenomenon was not unknown—but what caused it?

Shortly thereafter, in the winter of 1996-97, I got my first real insight into the connection between physical and mental bodies. My friend Ed Carter came to town to question me while I was in an altered state of consciousness—what we called having a session with The Guys Upstairs.

To adequately discuss talking to "the Guys Upstairs" would bring us a long way from the topic at hand. To put it in a nutshell: over the years I have developed access to an internal source of guidance. I don't "hear voices," or go into trance. The process is more like getting into a highly receptive state and saying whatever comes to mind. For all I know, it may be simply a means of bypassing the limitations of the conscious mind and tapping into deeper resources. It seems to be a natural human ability, available to all who trouble to develop it. I know dozens, if not scores, of people who do it equally routinely.

But on the day Ed arrived, I was not in great shape. For a couple of weeks, I had been coughing, a dry wracking cough, continuously, day and night. Since "talking to the guys" depended on my being able to get into a highly receptive state—which usually involved my lying down on a couch—I didn't know how well it would work. I was finding it hard even to *sit* quietly, let alone lie down! But I lay down to give it a try, and to my surprise my breathing quickly settled down, the coughing went away, and we went through a session lasting half an hour or so.

When the tape recorder clicked off at the end of one side of tape, and I got up to use the bathroom, Ed asked if I wanted him to ask them anything. The coughing had started again, immediately, so I said, "Yes, ask them why when I'm talking to them my breathing is fine, and as soon as we stop I'm coughing again." But before I even got to the bathroom I had the answer, which was confirmed when we resumed the session and asked: It's because our health is a ratio between our physical states and our mental states. Changing *either* the physical or mental side of the equation will change the ratio, and thus will bring us to a different state of health.

This has proved true in the years since. Even in the middle of a long-running asthma attack, I can breathe normally and comfortably, flat on my back, as long as we're doing a session with The Guys.

Clearly, something in those sessions involves mental states more than physical states, or my health wouldn't fluctuate so radically, so quickly. I have read, too, that people with multiple personalities may have one personality that is diabetic and another that is not. This seems like strong evidence that changing mental states change health by changing the mind-body ratio.

That's important, because it gives us two strings to our bow. Sometimes we will find it easier to work from the physical side (change of diet, or more exercise, or whatever); sometimes, from the mental side (make conscious efforts to avoid indulging in worry or anger, for instance). The side you work from depends on whether you're looking for quick change or permanent change.

Physical states change only slowly, over time. Mental states fluctuate. (In fact, fluctuating mental states is practically a definition of normal consciousness.) Changing your physical state will take time, but the change will tend to endure. When you change your mental state, the change will come quickly—sometimes instantly—but will be harder to hold.

I came into this life firmly convinced that the mind was the most important thing. Mental powers have always seemed to me self-evident, even if I couldn't quite remember how to obtain or cultivate them. And so I don't instinctively think in terms of using physical means to maintain physical health. Instead, my bias continuously tempts me to try to maintain my health through mental rather than physical effort, which certainly is doing things the hard way. Just as one would expect, this leaves me vulnerable to sudden fluctuations in health, and I don't advise it as a strategy. Do what I say, not what I do.

After decades of experience, it is clear to me that to some extent our physical health *is* under our own mental control. The degree of control differs for different people. To understand the variables involved, we need to discuss what I call Downstairs-you and Upstairs-you.

"Downstairs-you" is the part of yourself that you are most aware of, the part of you that lives in time and space. Those who identify themselves with the body identify themselves with only their Downstairs component.

Even those who think of themselves as comprising Body, Mind and Spirit may in practice be dealing only Downstairs. They may know that they are more than their physical body, but they may think of the body as the physical instrument, the mind as the thinking apparatus that controls the body, and the sprit as some non-physical component. In practice, this isn't all that different from believing only in the body, as if mind were a secretion of the brain and spirit were an illusion.

"Upstairs-you" means that part of yourself that lives beyond time and space, and hence is bounded by neither. This is the home of abilities and perceptions that are inexplicable in Downstairs-only terms. Thus, how much control over your health you have depends on how connected you are to your Upstairs components. I count five possible levels of relationship between the two—in essence, five levels of being.

The lowest level, which we might call *Downstairs Only*, includes those whose conscious minds are not at all in touch with the part of themselves functioning from beyond time and space. Such people have only the most indirect control over their own health. They can do the physical things that will have a physical result—maintaining a positive attitude, following sensible health rules—and not much else. Their best bet is to let the automatic mechanisms of the body operate automatically. If they have a physical problem, they will have to deal with it in physical terms, because they have such a limited tool chest.

Then there are those whose conscious minds are still dealing only Downstairs, but who are intuitively connected to their Upstairs component. These people instinctively know what they should do, what they should eat, and what helps or harms their health. Because their intuition and their everyday life are not in conflict, their natural habits will lead toward health. They will not be sick as often as those operating strictly Downstairs, and they will *seem* naturally lucky. That "luck" is actually the result of the fact that they have extra resources to call on. Call them *Connected Upstairs*.

A third level includes people who have gone beyond integrating their intuition, to become aware of modalities, such as, for instance, energy-healing work. They will be able to do more because they are moving their control to another level of being. They will be able to assist their own unconscious processes by focusing them. In other words, they will be loading the dice to get the result they want. These are the people who say "you need some healing energy here"—and are able to provide it. They may not know exactly how it works, but they know how to direct the energy, and that's enough. Call them, perhaps, *Dice Loaders*.

The fourth level we could perhaps term *Healers*. Those at this level have a greater, wider, deeper, surer, more conscious connection Upstairs, which puts control of their health ever more confidently into the hands of the wiser, more far-seeing part of themselves. At this level, you focus the energy through yourself, and it automatically fixes what needs fixing. I think that one of the things Jesus meant by "I and the father are one" was, "the energy runs through me without interference from me." This is the basis of all healing.

Ultimately, at the highest level of integration, are people we may call *Miracle Workers*. Jesus raised people from the dead, and said that we could learn to do everything he did, and more, and I see no excuse to doubt his word. And I take the fact that miracles are possible, and that *we* can grow to be able to perform them, as astounding good news.

This does not mean that taking away symptoms is always appropriate. The ability to suppress or remove symptoms can make things worse if it leads the sufferer to neglect dealing with the illness's underlying cause. For that matter, *even removing illness is not always appropriate.* So much depends on what the individual needs, and what kind of assistance s/he is ready and willing to accept. We forget, sometimes, that illness is a gift as well as an affliction. But at this fifth level, there is no effective limit to what may be done.

So at the moment, where are you on the scale stretching from Sensory Only to Miracle Worker? My guess is that (1)

LEVEL OF BEING	CHARACTERISTICS	DEGREE OF CONTROL	AVAILABLE RESOURCES
Miracles Workers	No distinctions	No barriers	Lower levels plus no known limits
Healers	Sure connection, Upstairs Control	Wiser self directs	Lower levels plus automatic direction
Dice Loaders	Relinquishing control	Can focus unconscious processes	Lower levels plus can direct energy
Connected Upstairs	Intuitively connected	Naturally "lucky"	Lower levels plus instinctive knowings
Downstairs Only	Aware only of time-space	Physical things, physical results	Automatic body mechanisms only

you probably don't *know* where you are, and (2) you don't realize that from one moment to the next you slide around on the scale.

I knew a man who habitually referred to himself as "ESP-thick," but once, when his infant child had a dangerous fever, he somehow knew that he could take it away, and he knew how to do it. He put his hand on the baby's head—and the fever went down. He would tell the story as though it were an inexplicable anomaly, but it seems straightforward enough to me. Under pressure of necessity, motivated by his intense love for his child, he tapped into an inner knowing that is normally inaccessible to him. His belief system ("I am ESP-thick") continually reminds him that regardless of whether others can conduct healing energies, surely he himself could not. It took the threat to his child's well-being to bring forth what was always there. Predictably, when the emergency left, the ability left with it. Or so he believes, and as long as he believes it, it will remain true.

So what about you? Take out a pad and pencil, and ask yourself if you have ever had an anomalous healing experience. Ask the question, then spend a few moments in a sort of daydreaming consciousness, so that things half-forgotten (or long forgotten) can rise to your mind's surface. Perhaps you will be surprised to realize that your life hasn't been quite as dull as you sometimes think! It wouldn't surprise me in the slightest.

Ask yourself:

- Do I believe that illness is ever useful? chosen? necessary?

- Do I know anyone who has exhibited healing powers?

- Do I know someone who has an amazing resistance to illness?

- Am I more open to intuition, or sensory evidence, or both?

- Have I ever done something I shouldn't have been able to do?

- Have I ever known something without evidence, not having any idea how I knew it?

- When I'm really sick, what do I trust? Conventional medicine? Energy medicine? Spiritual healing? Different things for different kinds of illnesses?

- Which level best represents where I am most of the time? Sensory Only? Intuitive only? Dice Loaders? Healer? Miracle Worker?

- How often do I function at a level higher or lower than my usual level ?

- What level would be my natural level if I had my preference?

As to that last question—getting what you want seems to depend mostly on how much you want it. First comes the knowledge that the abilities exist to be developed, then comes the belief—even if it is only a provisional belief—that you yourself can develop them. And, if even provisional belief is too much to ask at first, then at least the belief that until you try, you don't know for sure that you can't! Until recently, we were sort of automatically programmed to disbelieve. That is changing, and it would please me very much if this book helped push the change a little faster, a little farther.

Chapter 2

Four Assumptions

Which is more important to you, your world-view or your health? It may be that the world-view you have absorbed from the society around you is interfering with your control over your own health. Anything that remains unconscious rather than conscious affects our behavior without our knowing about it, as psychoanalysts and advertising agencies could testify. This is why society's shared assumptions are so hard to shake off. What everybody implicitly believes becomes invisible, self-evident, beyond question. We can't really judge submerged material until we bring it to the light of consciousness. Thus, bringing our society's tacitly accepted beliefs into consciousness is the only way we can attain our proper control over them. Once we do, some of what had seemed plain common sense will be seen as merely *one* way to see things, and perhaps not at all the most plausible way.

Please note, this is not a *political* statement. There's no use generalizing about who believes what. It is neither helpful nor necessary. If you don't share the following common assumptions, so much the better; you may skip to part two. If you *do* share them, or "sort of" share them, perhaps the following discussion will lead you to a more positive view of your possibilities. But there's no point in worrying about what other people believe. That's their problem.

I count four major commonly accepted assumptions that stand in the way of our taking greater charge of our own health. You may find that it takes some effort to give them a critical examination, as they may seem so obviously true. I assure you, it is worth the effort. Maybe you will look at them and continue to believe them. But perhaps once you really look at them, you will decide that the truth lies elsewhere. I urge you, take the risk. Again, what's more important to you, your world-view or your health?

The "mainstream" of our society unconsciously assumes that:

1. *Things sometimes "just happen."* Chance exists, and so do accidents and coincidences.

2. *Illness is externally caused.* We may become ill for reasons beyond our control, reasons that have nothing to do with our own life.

3. *Our physical, emotional, mental, and spiritual components are separate and distinct from one another.* That is, what happens to the body isn't necessarily related to what's going on with your emotional or mental life, let alone your spiritual life.

4. *The physical body is a mechanical system.* Thus, it may be effectively treated as though it were a machine, with chemical intervention (medicines), backed up by mechanical intervention (surgery) as needed.

I don't think any of those assumptions are true. My experience argues that in trying to correct or maintain your health, it is worthwhile to live believing just the opposite:

1. It is *not* true that things "just happen," or that chance, accidents, or coincidences really exist, regardless of appearances.

2. It is *not* true that we become ill for reasons that are separate from the rest of our lives. Illness (and health no less) expresses our inner condition.

3. It is *not* true that our physical, emotional, mental, and spiritual components are separate and distinct from one another.

4. It is *not* true that the physical body is a mechanical system.

Change those four unconscious assumptions and you wind up with a radically different picture of human health and life.

If chance, accident and coincidence exist in appearance only, then everything in your life is meaningful.

If illness expresses something in our inner condition, it may be quite valuable.

If your physical, spiritual, emotional and mental aspects are vitally interconnected, those interconnections may be of great use in understanding and overcoming illness, and hence in restoring or maintaining health.

And, finally, if you can communicate with your body and its organs, you can establish a feedback loop that will prove very powerful.

Rather than dwell on the negative, let's re-state these four negations as positive statements and look at them in order.

Everything is connected. I know it doesn't look like it, but it's true. Our internal lives and our external lives mirror each other, for the very good reason that they are two ways of viewing (and participating in) *the very same reality.*

This cannot be "proved" by logic. The only thing that will prove it for you will be your own experience. I strongly encourage you to start living your life *as if* everything were connected. Look for meaning behind what may at first seem to be mere coincidence. I cannot guarantee that you will begin to see the underlying unity of all the things in our lives, but I can guarantee this: You will never see that unity if you don't at least make the attempt to see life that way. Again, it is a matter not of *belief,* but of *absence of disbelief.* Be open to the possibility, and see what your life shows you.

We commonly assume that everything would be fine if nothing "bad" ever happened. But struggles bring growth. Health struggles, particularly, can have a spiritual aspect, and a mental aspect, as well as a purely physical aspect, and you can never know what might come of them. Maybe for a long time—maybe for your whole lifetime—it looks like nothing good is coming out of it. Still, you don't know.

And if we don't know about our own life struggles and illnesses, how much less can we know about another's! It's a very common mistake to look at somebody's life and— because we can see things about them that they themselves can't—assume that we know what they should do or what they should be. We look at their lives and think, "What *are* they doing? How can they be so foolish?" But even if this is true on a Downstairs level, it would rarely seem so straightforward seen from Upstairs. To put it simply, people don't do things without reason. They don't get themselves into emotional entanglements, they don't get themselves fired, they don't provoke problems with their health, without reason. But neither they nor you may have any idea what those reasons are. And perhaps neither they nor you have any business knowing.

We don't know, because we *can't* know. Perhaps whatever is being worked out has to do not only with life now but with life to come. (I don't say it does. I say, perhaps.) In the last analysis we are left either believing, or being unable to believe, that all is always well, which is what mystics consistently tell us.

Seth, as channeled by Jane Roberts in the latter half of the 20th century, stresses that we continually create our own bodies and use them as windows from which we look out into the world. But if this is so, why are we troubled with disease and illness? Why do we not have perfect health? For that matter, why are we overweight? Why do we lose our hair, or see it turn grey? We don't know.

Part of the answer may be the conflict between conscious creation and unconscious creation. The one either augments the other, or contradicts it. In fact, it often does both at once, augmenting one part, contradicting another part. If we consistently choose health—create health—we are healthy. If we choose ill-health—as we sometimes do, finding life insupportable—then we get that instead. But it is not that clearcut. You may not wish to have problems with your teeth, say, but if you think negatively of them, and have learned to expect them to give you trouble, you will not be disappointed. People say that tooth trouble stems from bad habits and from hereditary weaknesses, and if you believe it, it is so. But it is not the entire story.

In practical terms, not merely as a figure of speech, we have not one but four bodies, as a few minutes' thought and experimentation will show. Can you experience the mental, emotional, and energy bodies? Yes, you can. And it isn't hard.

You know you have a physical body because you experience it every moment. But unless you are a lot more conscious than I usually am, you experience the body as one undifferentiated mechanism that functions more or less automatically. But in actuality, it is a complicated set of interlocking intelligences. Two examples are the placebo effect, and a prospective father's sympathy pains. (And it shouldn't surprise you that both of these very telling indicators are derided by our materialistic, disconnected society.)

By now most people know, or think they know, what the placebo effect is. If you give people a sugar pill or similarly neutral substance that they believe is a medicine, a certain percentage will get well with no other treatment. This is sometimes seen as an indicator of people's gullibility, but I don't see much difference between people's reactions to placebos and their reactions to patent medicines—or to prescription medicines, for that matter. In all these cases, they are putting their faith in a physical substance to correct a health problem. Yet the placebo effect demonstrates that in at least a significant number of cases the *belief*, not the physical *substance*, is what cures. By rights, it ought to be called "the miracle effect."

And if in many cases it isn't the medicine but the belief that cures, how do we know but that those who received medicine also got better not because of the medicine but *because of their belief.* Energy healing doesn't work a hundred percent of the time. Neither do religious rites, or placebos, or surgery, or prescription medicines. I wonder how many medical procedures work mostly because people believe in them. We know this has been true in past generations, because we don't now believe in the medicines they believed in then. If it doesn't *always* work, what's going on when it *does* work? It's a fair question about energy healing and it's a fair question about conventional medicine.

As to sympathy pains, societies all over the world have reported the same phenomenon. A woman suffering labor pains; the baby's prospective father experiencing pains just like hers—sympathy pains—for no physical reason. Many people assume that because he is not actually carrying a baby, this phenomenon isn't real and couldn't be real. But I have no doubt that it *can* happen, because I think I know *why* it happens, and what it represents. In the years since I began helping others to heal, I have often experienced a different form of sympathy pains, and I find them very useful.

Part of helping others to heal involves "connecting" with them. When I do that, I often feel pain in the places where they feel pain, and feel it (so far as I can tell) with the same intensity and "flavor" as they do. This is enormously helpful, as it tells me where to focus our efforts. It occurred to me one day that a prospective father's sympathy pains may be exactly the same thing. Being in close sympathy with the prospective mother of his child, the prospective father feels what she is feeling. At least, maybe.

Here we come to the nub of it. And the first step is to have an in-the-body experience.

How well do you know your body? How often do you check to see if you are *in* your body? That may sound like a joke, or a meaningless statement, but in fact I suggest that many of us are riding around in unfamiliar vehicles. We don't relate to them even as well as we do with, say, our cars. We don't do the maintenance, we don't watch the gauges, we've never looked in the owner's manual (nor do we know where to find it) and we often think of them primarily as useful nuisances—necessary, but often troublesome and sometimes expensive to maintain. Maybe we like them, maybe we don't. Maybe we like to tinker with them, tuning them up for higher performance perhaps, or maybe we just want them to work when we need them.

Sound familiar?

Suppose that instead of treating our bodies like cars (*rented* cars, at that!) we began treating them the way affectionate owners treat their pets? How would our lives be different?

For one thing, we would recognize that we are dealing with separate intelligent beings with their own needs and desires, and their own personalities. We would realize that for best results, we must adapt our interactions to take their nature into account. Try herding cats! Try making dogs into vegetarians! Perhaps it can be done, but it isn't ever going to be done very well, and anyway, what's the point?

I know that it may be a new idea, but it isn't any secret that each part of the body has its own intelligence. We often think of ourselves as brains directing bodies, as though the brain were the intelligence and the rest of the body merely a very complicated, very precise machine. That's a vastly over-simplified model that overlooks what has been discovered in our time. Take the heart, for instance. Did you know that the heart is laid down in the fetus *before* the brain? Did you realize that the heart sends more electrical information *to* the brain than it receives *from* the brain? Did you know the recipients of heart transplants have sometimes changed in ways that made them more closely resemble the heart donor?

Nor is it a matter of merely expanding our concept of a control system to include brain *and* heart. The Chinese believe that the soul is in the stomach. Do you suppose that they have any reason for that? Should we factor that in, too? Beyond that, we have to factor in layer upon layer of complexity. The body has chemical signaling systems, and electrical ones. The ductless glands appear to be connected to what Eastern metaphysical systems call the chakras. Every subsystem—every organ—comes equipped with feedback mechanisms that keep the whole system functioning in a necessarily interconnected way.

And each organ accomplishes quite specialized tasks. What the kidneys do is quite different from what the lungs do. Does it not stand to reason that what the kidneys *know* is therefore quite different from what the lungs *know*? (Lawyers aren't automatically qualified to drive railroad trains just because they're well trained as lawyers.) Until relatively recently we thought that all these sub-systems were directed by the brain. Many people still think so. I suspect that the fact that each organ knows what it has to do implies that each organ has its own organizing intelligence.

So the first step is to recognize that the body as a unit is an intelligence, and the second step is to realize that it may equally well be thought of as a collection of interconnecting intelligences. All cells are created the same way, just as all people start out as zygotes, but that does not make cells or people interchangeable once they have become specialized by a certain amount of experience. One zygote grows up to be a salesman, another becomes a farmer. One cell becomes part of a lung, another becomes part of a muscle. Salesmen aren't farmers, and lungs aren't muscle tissue. (Yes, people can change careers—can even be cross-trained—but so much for analogy.)

The fact is, experience has shown me that we *can* and *should* communicate with different parts of our bodies just as if we were talking to another individual. As the man said about free will, theory may be against it, but experience is for it. It works. Even if my understanding of why it works is wildly wrong—if it works, who cares? What good can come of an understanding that leads you away from greater control of your health? And what harm can come from a *mis*understanding, if it leads *toward* greater control of your health? Theory is all well and good, but who in his right mind would prefer useless theory over helpful practice if it were a choice of one or the other? Sure, it would be nice to be certain, but in the meantime, it's nice to know something useful.

Part Two

TAKING
CHARGE

Chapter 5

From Helpless Victim to Consulting Detective

Doctors, chiropractors, massage therapists, nurses—health professionals of all kinds—spend years learning how the body works. Think of the labor involved even to learn anatomy! Then you have to learn the specialized functions of each part of the body, and how the parts function together, and how they may malfunction, and what you can and cannot do about such malfunctions. It isn't any surprise that medicine is less one discipline than a collection of specialties. There is so much to know!

I have great respect for those who do the work of learning the body as an intricately interconnected system. If I offer a different approach, it's because this way works for those of us who do not have specialized medical training. We forget, sometimes, that medical resources, like all resources, are limited. Everyone who can learn to keep himself healthy frees resources for others for whom medical attention may be a matter of life and death.

My way is to find and deal with the *deepest* causes of the illness, the causes that are rooted most deeply in life. Deal with what you might call the metaphysical causes, and the physical problem goes away as though by a miracle. Not every cause can be removed, and for all we know, perhaps sometimes it is in our higher interest that not every "problem" be removed. But you may be surprised how many things can be remedied or alleviated. You can use it on yourself, and you can also use it to help others help themselves, provided that they do not have overwhelming resistance to the concept. This isn't the only way to approach health and wellness, but it does have the advantage of being accessible to all who are not prejudiced against it.

It is a four-step process.

1. *Ascertain that you are ready to be rid of the illness.* You might think that this is automatically true, but experience will surprise you. When you start thinking of illness as *part of* your life pattern, rather than as *an interruption* to the life pattern, you will find it easier to see that at certain times in our life we seem to need certain illnesses, and at other times we are ready to shrug them off. When you are sure, or anyway pretty sure, that you are ready to move on from this illness, proceed to step two.

2. *Personify the illness or the part of the body that is experiencing or causing the illness.* Ask: "How are you serving me by having me experience this?" Again, this assumes that the illness is *part of the pattern*, not an *interruption* of the pattern. It assumes that your body is doing its best to give you what it

thinks you want. Before you overrule your body, know why it's doing what it's doing. Otherwise you're setting yourself up for the same illness to pop up again, or for another illness to pop up in its place, as the body continues to try to serve you in the way that it thinks you want it to.

3. *Sincerely and openly wait for the body to respond to your question.* The answer may come in the form of words, or pictures, or simply "a knowing." You asked the question: Now *listen to the answer!* Don't be surprised if at first it doesn't seem to make sense. It comes from a region that may be far removed from your ordinary conscious thought. When you get an answer, listen to it. Be sure you know what is being said, even if at first you don't know what it means. *Feel* the response. Weigh it, live with it.

4. *When you know what you got, react to it appropriately.* In my experience, the response you get will result either from an outdated situation, or a present situation. Tailor your own response accordingly.

a) *An outdated situation.* Anything unconscious has no time, by definition. Emotions that are not brought to consciousness are as alive and present as the day they were first experienced. Thus, automatic reactions—including illness and injury—can remain in being long after the situations have passed that called them forth. For example, I injured my back when I was nineteen years old, and thereafter for more than thirty years, my back was continually subject to re-injury, because the place that had been injured held itself rigid rather than moving as it should. Finally a massage therapist coaxed the tissue into relaxing, but had I known then what I know now, I would have talked to that part of my back and told it two things. First, I would have assured it that I would not repeat the carelessness that had resulted in injury. More important, I would have told it that the way it was holding itself was resulting in re-injury. When you find yourself dealing with an outdated situation, speak to the part of your body that is causing the problem and tell it, sincerely, not sarcastically, "Thank you for working to assist me. I do not need this kind of assistance. Time has passed and the old situation has gone."

b) *A present situation.* Sometimes a physical problem really does serve you, often by protecting something else or by preventing you from doing something that it thinks would cause harm. For example, one day when I was visiting a friend, he said he had to go outdoors to be sure his wife (an avid gardener) wasn't overdoing, as this always brought on a painful bout of arthritis. Listening to instinct, I asked her if she would be open to a little energy work. She was. I asked her to personify her shoulder and ask how it was serving her by aching with arthritis. She went within for a moment or two, and then somewhat sheepishly said, "It stops me from overdoing." So there was our answer. I suggested that she make a deal with her shoulder. Whenever she was in danger of overdoing, the shoulder would give her just a twinge, just enough to get her attention. Her part of the bargain was that when she felt the twinge, she would stop. She made the deal and to the best of my knowledge has not had problems with her shoulder in the years since. When you realize that a problem deals with a real situation, say, "Thank you for working to assist me. Let's make an agreement. When [causal factor x] exists, twitch the little finger of my right hand [or whatever] to remind me what I should [or shouldn't] do."

c) *Undetermined.* When the answers you get don't make sense, make a real effort to be sure that there is no sense to be found. Often, there is. But sometimes, there's just no figuring out what's going on. I was doing the "ask the body" routine with a friend who was suffering from many pains, and the answer she got was that the pains were intended to help her lose unwanted weight. I suppose you might consider that such an answer sort of fits into category (b), but it seems to me that this kind of logic, you can do without. Say with gratitude (for its intent, if not for its logic!), "Thank you for working to assist me. I do not need this kind of assistance."

Our physical tissues hold memories.

This may be a new idea to you, but I take it as long since proven. Body workers such as massage therapists report that their clients sometimes relive old mental or emotional traumas when tissues associated with those traumas are manipulated.

Psychologist Wilhelm Reich discovered and analyzed body "armoring" decades ago. The assumption has been amply demonstrated in many places. Let's see what this fact means to us.

Given that specific tissues can hold specific emotions and memories, one useful way to access those memories is to visualize emotions and memories as though they were laid out on a map of the body. And we can make different maps for different uses.

One map of a given country may show rail lines, and a second natural resources, and a third political boundaries. Same territory, different maps, because simplification and specialization make for ease of analysis. We can do the same thing with "maps" of our mental and emotional life. The difference is that mental and emotional body "maps," unlike maps of resources or political boundaries, share the intelligence of the emotional and mental reality they map. This makes them very useful as a feedback mechanism.

Let's start with the mental and emotional bodies. You might argue that mind and emotion are two aspects of the same thing, and I wouldn't care to argue that they aren't. But for our purposes it is as well to consider them separately. After all, in the final analysis everything is all part of one thing anyway. Mind, emotion, energy, physical matter—where are you going to find an absolute separation? We make arbitrary divisions for convenience. But they are not absolutes.

So, the mental body. Your mind is more than your brain, and serves a wider purpose. We sometimes think of our brains as computers. But actually, it is more productive to think of the entire system as the computer. The *brain* is the physical structure and the operating system. The *mind* is the software that uses the operating system. It *runs* on the system; it is not a *product* of the system.

Similarly, the emotional body. Emotions are *conveyed* by the chemical signaling system, and perhaps may be *simulated* by manipulation of that system, but they are not merely the automatic product of chemical reactions.

Making a map of the physical, emotional, mental, and energetic bodies is a trick I learned years ago at The Monroe Institute, in Virginia. I don't know that the institute invented the technique but it certainly puts it to good use.

It's simple. Imagine yourself standing in front of a mirror. Get a good sense of yourself. Now copy that image, unchanged, and split it off to one side. Color the copy blue, and call it the mental body. Make another copy; color it green, and call it the emotional body.

Now concentrate on the blue, mental body, and bear in mind, this map was created by your imagination, following your direction to accurately portray your underlying mental reality. That means it is able to portray things *you don't consciously know*. That is a good part of its value to you. *Consider it an active feedback device, reflecting your underlying mental reality.*

Look at the overall color, and see if the blue looks "healthy" to you over all. See if the map has dull spots in it. See if it has bright spots. Try to change any dull spots or bright spots so that the entire body map is one smooth healthy color. If one or another part of the map calls itself to your attention, give some loving attention to that part of the map, and intend that the corresponding part of your body benefit. Keep on until the entire body map is a healthy even color without hot spots or dull spots, and without any areas calling for your attention.

You see how useful this body map concept? *You don't even have to know what you are working on!* It doesn't matter. The body knows. What you are doing (at least, *my* conception of what you are doing) is coupling the focusing ability of the conscious mind and the maintenance power of the subconscious mind. This assists in creating or maintaining normal health.

Now deal with the emotional body in the same way. Examine the green color, look over the entire map, and send energy where it needs to go. Brighten dull spots and smooth out hot spots until you are left with a map of your emotional body that is a smooth, healthy attractive green. Pay attention to areas that seem to want attention. You don't have to know *what* and you don't have to know *why*. Just give yourself the loving attention and support that you would give your child.

Treating the energetic body is similar, but just a bit different. I suppose you could do exactly the same thing with the energy body that you did with the mental and emotional bodies—seek to make the color even and healthy, without hot spots and dull spots—and leave it at that. Yet whenever I do the exercise, I add another step, and do it first. (But others have other routines. Do what feels right.)

I envision the energetic body less as a copy of the physical body, and more as a translucent container, a bag filled with the energy that we use in our daily life. I try to visualize it as vibrant and glowing, full of energy. If I can't, I know we're in trouble. First I look for rips or holes that would be letting the energy leak out of the container. When I find them, I smooth them together and sort of butter them back into place so that the "fabric" is again unbroken and healthy. Only when I am convinced that there are no leaks do I look for hot spots and dull spots and other problems.

I can practically hear you saying, "It's only a visualization, for crying out loud! Visualizations don't develop rips!" Right. But wrong, too. Visualizations are communication through metaphor. The subconscious mind doesn't do words very well but it's *very* good with visuals, and symbols. (Think what proportion of your dreams are words as opposed to the proportion that is symbol.) So long as you and your subconscious both know what you're wanting to accomplish, why shouldn't the visualization be accurate? Trust it.

Chapter 4

Reprogramming Your Robots

The techniques already outlined will work much of the time, but not always. Sometimes what seems a simple physical problem does not respond. Such cases may be inviting you to deal with quite different problems, often unsuspected. You may have encountered one of the mechanisms that I call robots.

(After initially writing earlier drafts of this manuscript, I realized that I picked up the concept of mental robots from my friend, British author Colin Wilson, who used it frequently. However, although it is the same word, we are referring to different processes. He was discussing how our everyday consciousness becomes somewhat mechanical in repetitious circumstances. My use of the term is considerably different, as will appear.)

My friend Nancy Ford and I discovered robots a few years ago—January 8, 2008, a day to be remembered. She and I had known each other for a few years, and from time to time I had been able to help her free her shoulder joints, usually after she had overworked in her garden. On this day, though, she brought me a much more difficult problem. Overworking, she had injured her wrist in a way that resulted in the last three fingers of her left hand dragging. She didn't ask for help until a year had gone by with no improvement. Then her guidance suggested that perhaps I could help.

Well, I did everything I knew how to do, and nothing worked. The best we could achieve was a very slight, very temporary improvement, and then the situation would revert. It was puzzling, not because I expect to be able to fix anything that comes my way, but because—well, it was just fishy, somehow. And then out of the blue I "heard" that the physical problem was being held so that she would not neglect to address one or more underlying *emotional* problems!

So then we began exploring, and that was the beginning of a journey that went on for months, then years, in the course of which we discovered the connection between the unconscious mind, and the things we are aware of, and the mechanisms—call them robots—that connect the two.

It's worth remembering that life doesn't really fit into categories. Everything interconnects. Or, you could equally well say that there's only *one everything*, which looks different from different viewpoints. If you look at something one way, it's physical. Look at it another way, and it's mental. Another way, and it's spiritual. You are looking at *one* thing, not three things. What's changing is the way you look at it. That probably sounds pretty abstract, but it gives us the key to correcting problems that are intractable when dealt with as if they were *only* physical, or *only* emotional, or *only* spiritual.

At first I thought of robots as dysfunctional, if not malign, but I have come to realize that they are how we live our lives. We use them to drive our cars and tie our shoes and do any of the countless things we do more or less auto-matically. Remember how hard it was to learn how to drive a car? Remember learning to touch-type, or square dance, or speak a foreign language? Anything we've ever learned to do fluently, we've learned to do automatically. We've handed it over to a robot, which does it for us better than we could do it consciously. (This is what Colin Wilson was referring to.) They free us to do other things.

The problem is that unless and until we consciously contact them and update their files, so to speak, they continue to do what they were programmed to do, no matter how circumstances may have changed. The automatic reaction that serves a 7-year-old is likely to cause a lot of trouble if it continues to function in a 27-year-old, not to mention a 57-year-old! But an unconscious tool can't reprogram itself; that's up to us. Until we do, it will continue following orders given, perhaps, long ago, far away, by a very different being.

A robot following obsolete reprogramming is something like the definition of a weed as "a plant out of place." It isn't good or bad; it just needs to be managed. The robots are not the problem. The programming is the problem. Once you reprogram a given robot or complex of robots, you restore *flow*. You aren't frozen.

To reprogram involves only two things: analysis and communication. But if you are to understand the what and the why and the how of these two steps, first we must take something of a detour.

To understand how I deal with robots, you have to keep in mind the assumptions I work from.

First—everything has intelligence.

From the lowest collection of cells to the highest organization that exists (whatever that may be), I have never yet experienced any advantage in assuming that something with which I was interacting did *not* have intelligence.

Second—the permanence of time.

Here in 3-D, we experience time like this: "The past is gone, the future is not yet created. Only the present moment exists, and it is continually being created and destroyed, moment by moment, as we go along. Thus it is impossible for us to interact with our "past" or "future" selves: They don't exist!" We experience time this way, not because we're doing something wrong, but because the fact that we experience time that way makes certain things possible that are not possible in the non-physical world. (See my book, *The Cosmic Internet*.) Nonetheless, it isn't true. Past, present, and future are not what they appear, because *time* is not how it appears. Every moment of time exists; it doesn't come into being, it doesn't change into something else, it doesn't cease to exist. All time exists, regardless where we are in time, in the same way that all geography exists, regardless where we are in space. All moments of time exist forever.

Third—the non-physical nature of mind.

It is true that our *brains* are physical, and have to follow the laws of the physical universe. But our *minds* are not our brains. Our minds express *through* our brains, but the two are not the same thing. Because our minds obey the laws of non-physical existence rather than the physical world, they are not bound to the present moment, but may range freely between past and future, and between minds in different bodies.

Fourth—the reality of internal guidance.

We all have access to guidance, by which I mean wisdom available to us for the asking. Our materialist society downplays the idea, because it can't figure out a mechanism for it, but guidance is easily experienced, and is probably experienced more often, and in more ways, than it is noticed. It can come in so *many* forms: Hunches, knowings, stray thoughts, so-called coincidences. It comes in a million forms, and it's always there, but it's up to us whether or not we take advantage of it. As far as I can tell, the only things necessary for us to receive guidance are consciousness and an open heart. And that combination—consciousness and an open heart—is precisely what you need in order to achieve internal freedom. It's how you reprogram your robots.

Fifth—the fact that external life reflects the psyche.

Often it seems that there is little or no connection between our own internal world and what we see around us. But a little experience of looking at the external world for clues to your internal world will show you that in fact they do connect, often in surprising ways. When we interact with the world, we may become aware of the unconscious parts of ourselves, what psychologist Carl Jung called the shadow. The shadow isn't necessarily better or worse than our conscious self, but it *is* hidden, until something activates it. Then we do and say things that surprise us, and we think, "That wasn't really me." When our shadow side becomes alive, it controls us. As

Jung put it, "until you make the unconscious conscious, it will direct your life, and you will call it fate." And how would we ever experience it, if the world around us did not bring it forth? A man who had a real problem with women, and didn't know it, might spend his entire life in a locked room, never seeing a woman, and the problem would never manifest, so he would never suspect it. But it would continue to exist. Mostly, we know what the world reflects for us. If not for the world around us, we'd never know who we really are.

These assumptions are the result of experience which is hard for me to explain in their absence. For instance, (1) we often deal with the intelligence behind a given physical organ, or joint, or system; (2) some of the intelligences we communicate with are connected to what are called "past" or "future" lives; (3) interaction with guidance, and other non-physical intelligences is so much a part of this work that it would be impossible to do if it were impossible to maintain such contact; (4) call them hunches, intuitions, beginner's luck, chance—label it how you will—everyone who does this kind of work knows that we proceed on more than mere logic or reasoning; and (5) the interconnection between inner and outer world is the key, as much as any other single thing. And the implications of this last requires a little practical explanation.

The easiest way to describe the right way to use the world to show us our shadow side is to describe the wrong ways. Here are three things we must not do, if we wish to use the world to illustrate the parts of ourselves that are hidden from us. Naturally, all three are things we do constantly.

- First, *blame others.* That puts us into helpless victim-hood. Since it isn't our fault, it doesn't call for any corrective action on our part.

- Second, *make excuses.* This amounts to blaming our circumstances. It shores up our story, and again, it keeps us stuck where we are.

- Third, *deny any meaningful connection* between what happened to us and what we are. This is a different way of blaming our circumstances, using the concept of bad luck.

The three strategies—blaming others, blaming excuses, and blaming luck—all accomplish the same vital task. They prevent us from actually understanding what's going on, lest we realize that we need to change.

And that brings us back to robots.

Now, bearing in mind those assumptions about the world, let's proceed to the actual process of reprogramming. It's a two-step process: First comes analysis (Where did this particular robot come from? Why is it doing what it's doing?) and then comes communication (How do we contact the robot and let it know what we want it to do?).

Analysis is not a matter of dry intellectual reasoning, and you don't put yourself on the couch, either. It's more like fishing, at least the way I do it. Say you have a thumb that keeps jamming, for no obvious reason. I ask you to ask your thumb if it is holding an awareness for you. Maybe something comes to you and maybe it doesn't, but surprisingly often something does come—*provided*—provided that you let come whatever comes, not censoring things that "don't make sense" or "aren't relevant." The keys usually don't seem to make sense, at first blush. Why would they? If they immediately made sense, chances are you would have let them surface long before. A variant on this technique is that perhaps I ask you and the answer comes to me rather than to you. That may be valid, but has to be treated a little more carefully, a little tentatively. External solutions are not necessarily wrong, but as a rule, we are each our own best authority on ourselves.

Once we identify the connection between the physical problem and the hidden problem it is holding the place for, we need to communicate with the robot to tell it to change. This does not mean telling it what it "should" do, and it does not mean lecturing it, or throwing logic at it, let alone upbraiding it. It means you sinking into the feeling place from which the robot was originally programmed, and then thanking it for its help and expressing what you want from this point on.

Sometimes one time is all it takes, but sometimes one condition will have more than one root, and will have to be addressed repeatedly. And sometimes, conditions return after having been dealt with successfully. If this happens, there's no point in becoming discouraged. You did it once, probably you can do it again. And, chances are, every time you need to do it again, you'll learn something.

Everybody has heard the cliché that says that problems are opportunities. So they are. Using this technique, you can reshape your life on an on-going basis, making it more what you want it to be. You find a problem, you fix the problem, and that changes you and you proceed from that new point. Nothing but death brings an end to problems, but each problem surmounted brings you nearer to what you want to be.

A few things to remember:

• First, to do this work, you must be *present*. Whenever you wake up, start again, and don't beat yourself up for having fallen asleep (i.e., living automatically).

• Second, remember that everyone and everything in your life can help you to become more aware of who you really are. That's why they're in your life.

• Third, *do* the work, don't just think about how to think about it.

• Fourth, withdraw your projections, so that you can see. Don't blame others, don't blame life. Look for the connection between what happens to you and who you really are.

• Fifth, remember that convincing others is neither necessary nor even possible. As always, your example will speak louder than your words.

• Finally, remember that nothing that happens to you can be without meaning. Live the way we are meant to live, joyously and free.

Chapter 5

Imagination as a Tool of Perception and Cure

Everything in this book proceeds from the assumption that our subconscious mind (loosely so-called) runs the body. It coordinates the various specialized organs, it juggles priorities, and it provides an emergency response. Both in maintaining health and in overcoming illness or injury, the subconscious mind does the work. So, if we have a health problem, it's the subconscious mind we need to deal with.

The subconscious is powerful but—by definition—not *conscious*. It has its routines, and it continues with them until something calls forth other reactions. That "something" can be an emergency of some sort, but it can also be *us*. To affect the body, interact with the subconscious. How? The easiest, most effective way, is simple visualization, because the subconscious mind seems to respond best to pictures. And that involves using imagination as a tool of perception and manipulation.

Visualizing and morphing works well for specific localized problems, especially when you are working with the assistance of others. In fact, dealing with a specific problem is almost too easy to describe. It may sound like nothing. All I can say is, try it. First you visualize the condition you want to address, then you morph the visualization to be the way you want it to be. That's all there is to it.

Say you have a sore throat. Call up a picture of what a sore throat feels like *to you*. You might make a mental picture of a hollow tube of red, scratchy skin. Don't worry about the picture being accurate, or even recognizable. In fact, the best picture may be a cartoon, because it emphasizes just what you want to emphasize. You want to get the attention of the subconscious mind and inform it of a problem you want it to work on. That's all you're trying to accomplish. Whatever picture works for you, use it.

Then, when you have that picture firmly in mind, visualize that red scratchy skin changing, flowing gently into whatever your mental image is of healthy throat tissue. Smooth, pink skin, maybe. Like the original visualization, the morphed visualization doesn't have to be accurate; it needs to communicate to the subconscious mind, which will do the rest.

The most important limitation on the effectiveness of this technique is not how well you can visualize, but how well you can bring yourself to overcome the things you have been taught. You may have serious internal resistances to overcome. Visualizing and morphing may seem silly to you. It isn't easy to risk seeming foolish (even if only in our own eyes) but it is necessary. If you can't risk hoping that this technique will help you—then it can't. If you *can* risk it, it *can* help. Again, it's as simple as that.

It's a reckless generalization, but I'd say that all illness may be regarded as the result of some blockage somewhere. Remove the blockage, remove the cause of the illness.

Too simple? Probably, but let's think about cause and effect.

Every effect has both immediate causes (symptoms) and underlying causes. Sometimes it is appropriate to deal with symptoms: When you are in danger of going into diabetic shock, you have to deal with the immediate cause *right now,* or you may not live long enough to go any further. But ultimately, if you want to be well, you have to deal with underlying causes.

And how, if you are not a physician, do you deal with the underlying causes of disease? Or, to put the same question in a more positive way, how do you promote the underlying causes of health?

The answer is, you use visualization to remove the underlying causes of whatever health problems you have, regardless whether you are aware of the causes—*and regardless whether you are even aware of the problems.* Thus, you need not know how the body maintains itself.

Physicians, osteopaths, chiropractors, massage therapists, and other medical professionals spend years learning the body in great detail, so that they may know how to intervene to fix specific problems. The amount of knowledge needed to understand the body as a system made up of interconnecting systems is so large that no one could absorb it all. That's why we have specialists. But if you need not know *how* things go wrong, you can skip anatomy and physiology and chemistry and all. If you move back to the underlying causes, everything simplifies out. *You do not need to understand how your body systems work.* You only need to know to communicate with them, to assist them to do what they do.

For the hard of hearing: *You do not need to understand how your body systems work.*

Can you see how powerful this technique is? How foolproof? How proactive? How safe? At the same time, it has limits. It definitely won't work for those who won't give it a try. It won't necessarily help with immediate causes. And it won't necessarily heal everything.

Here is a simple meditation for maintaining the health of your physical, mental, emotional, and energetic bodies.

In doing this exercise, some people visualize themselves as one body; others visualize four bodies stacked one inside the other. Still others see four bodies holding hands in a circle. Doesn't matter, do what pleases you at the moment. (Over time, you may find that you sometimes prefer one and other times prefer another. And if you prefer to always do the same thing in the same way, that's fine too. Who would have the right to tell you how it "must" be done?)

Get into a comfortable sitting position and close your eyes. Take a few slow deep breaths, briefly holding your breath after you breathe in, and again after you breathe out. Relax. Imagine yourself standing under a waterfall, with the river of life and health flowing through you and around you. These waters represent our invisible support from the other side. They flow through us day and night, a silent unfailing support that we are rarely or maybe never aware of. The waters flow over you, and around you, and *through* you, penetrating every cell. There is so much water that you couldn't possibly take "more than your share." All you want is there for you, and you have an inborn right to all you need.

See the water coming down just as quickly or as slowly as seems right. There's nothing wrong with seeing it coming down in slow motion, and nothing wrong with seeing it moving sometimes slowly, sometimes quickly. You are not imitating nature; you are creating a visualization.

See the waters entering at the top of your head, and smoothly flowing down *through* your body, from head to toes. As you follow the fall of the waters, set your intent for the flow to gently, quietly, but effectively erode away any blockages that have accumulated in any of the four bodies.

In the physical body, blockages may be the result of past injuries or diseases. In the emotional body, they may be the unhealed result of past traumas. In the mental body, they may appear as prejudices, or systematic distortions in our ability to think and perceive. In the energetic body, they may appear as dull spots or hot spots, where we are either too insensitive or too sensitive to external input, or may appear as rips or tears through which our life energy "leaks," leaving us depleted.

During the course of the meditation, you may receive ideas or insights into the causes of various problems, not all of them physical. That's all well and good, and you should file those ideas away for later examination—but don't let them interfere with the actual process itself. During the meditation, do the meditation.

Hold your attention on the waters flowing smoothly down through your body. Watch—but don't interfere. Observe where the waters seem to get stuck. Set your intent that whatever obstacles hold up the water will be overcome. But don't cease to observe the flow of the waters down your body. When you have followed the flow down through your feet, begin again at the top of your head and follow it down.

Do this as long as seems appropriate, and stop when you feel like stopping. Much more important than how long you do this exercise is how often you do it. The more often, the better, even if it's only a minute or two at a time.

If you don't resonate to the waterfall, or if you find it hard to visualize standing under a waterfall when you are lying down, it's just as easy to imagine yourself lying down in a stream or a river, with your head toward the source of the flow. Imagine the water flowing down through your body in the same way as you would under a waterfall, and watch in the same way.

If the idea of being suffused with water doesn't work for you, try visualizing yourself in a field of light, the light beams scouring your body in the same way. Or try other things. One of my friends visualizes one of those shower heads that you hold in your hand, and uses it to direct the water to problem areas. Be creative.

That's the meditation, and that's the way I explain it to myself. As to how it really works—who knows? One theory is that concentrating our attention on the waters and obstructions calls those obstacles to the attention of the subconscious mind, which does the moment-to-moment work of maintaining the body. My preferred theory is that our physical body is laid down on an energy-body template, and once we adjust the energy body, the physical body readjusts itself to match the corrected template. But this is only theory, and, really, who cares? What matters is that it works.

This meditation is aimed at helping you to recognize and deepen your connection with all aspects of the seen and unseen world. Imagine yourself lying comfortably outdoors, in some surroundings that you like. I imagine myself in the desert, lying in a shallow hole dug to match my body, with a mat under me to keep out the sand, and a blanket over me for warmth. Choose whatever appeals to you, but here is mine.

> Get into a comfortable position and close your eyes. Take a few slow deep breaths, briefly holding your breath after you breathe in, and again after you breathe out. Relax. Imagine yourself lying on the land, looking up at the sky. You are safe, warm and comfortable. Is it daytime? Night time? Observe— and then close your eyes and *feel.* Beneath you the earth extends thousands of miles to its center. Feel the earth beneath you. Feel how you extend into the earth and are a part of the earth.

Now looking upward at the sky, extend upward. Feel yourself extending upward into the sky, and this is part of you too.

Extend in all directions on the surface of the earth, feeling your oneness with the earth. *Feel* that you are a part of the earth. It is not an inanimate host, but a living being, and you are a part of it. Feel that participation.

Now, holding that feeling of connection with the entire physical world, feel your connection to all the other living beings on this living planet. The animals of the land, the sea, and the air are all part of your family, and how much closer to you are the thousands of millions of humans. Feel that connection.

And when you have extended to encompass our entire physical life, extend to the other side of life, to the unseen part of us that lives outside time and space. Embrace that part of yourself, and know that you are not an orphan in the universe.

As with the previous exercise, do this one for as long as seems appropriate, and stop when you feel like stopping, and do it when you are so moved.

Part Three

LIVING
RIGHT

Chapter 6

Intuitive Knowing

Everything we need to know to heal ourselves or to help others to heal themselves is to be found in the world's scriptures. That's why they were put there. This shouldn't be a surprise. What *should be* a surprise is how little we use what we have been given.

An old joke says that the churches are filled with Christians who want to go to heaven, but don't want to die to get there. What if they are misunderstanding what Jesus meant? Jesus said, "The kingdom of God is within you." That doesn't sound much like "wait till you're dead and hope you get to heaven." Similarly, Jesus said, "I have come that you may have life and have it more abundantly." I think he meant "life more abundantly" not merely *after we die*, but *now*.

"Life more abundantly" means more than good health, but if you think that good health is not part of "life more abundantly," I can only congratulate you on having escaped (or risen above) chronic illness, substantial disability, or serious injury. You will notice that Jesus is not on record as ever having refused to heal anyone willing to be healed.

Neither do I recall him casting stones and saying that some-one "deserved" to suffer.

Now, I know that it's jarring to see casual references to Jesus and scriptures in a book on health and healing yourself. But think how much is to be learned from scriptures. It is true that knowledge is gained from direct experience. But in order to *get* that experience, sometimes we need guideposts, and in this case scriptures provide them. Jesus is the perfect model for me of someone bringing forth the higher self while still in the body—or, to put it into conventional religious terms, living by conforming our will to God's.

All the world's scriptures have equivalent passages—*because they are each trying to tell us what we need to know to live our lives.* Regardless what religious tradition you come from, I suggest to you that if you will read your scriptures as instructions aimed at educating, rather than as legal manu-als aimed at enforcing compliance, you will be surprised how differently they read. When we come to the day that people use scriptures as guidebooks to fuller life, rather than as texts to be memorized against an afterlife final exam, we will see religion transformed into something much closer to what it should be, and, for that matter, what science should be, too: A religion that respects and investigates and teaches spiritual *facts*! A science that is rooted in spiritual values! This will be the basis for a whole new civilization, and it cannot come too soon.

The point of this digression is this. Jesus said that the entire law and the prophets were contained in the command to do two things:

1. Love God with your whole being, and

2. Love your fellows as yourself.

Well, if you want health, if you want to help others heal, you need do two things.

1. You must learn to trust the knowledge that "comes to you," and

2. You must come from your heart.

To my mind, that's just what Jesus said. You must develop and use your intuition, and you must be love.

The greatest help I received in connecting with my healing abilities came when a friend told me to stop apologizing.

I had been learning to work with people for about a decade, feeling my way, working totally intuitively, usually not knowing what I was going to do or why I did it.

What I had learned about healing came from techniques picked up at The Monroe Institute, and two weekend courses, Reiki I, which taught techniques to hands-on healing, and Reiki II, which taught distant healing, But I didn't use either set of techniques very long. Both seemed unnecessarily complicated compared to what I knew from Monroe Institute techniques, and from—somewhere. Some other part of me knew things that "conscious-I" did not.

I could trust, pretty easily, when I was the only one involved. After all, that's what listening to guidance amounts to, openness and trust. But I found it harder to trust when working on others. Trying to heal others (or, more accurately, to help them find their way back to the healthy state) seemed like tightrope-walking without a net. So, as I was working on somebody, every time I would move my hands to another part of their energy body, I would say, in effect, "I don't know why I'm doing this, but my hands seem to want to." Finally one day my friend Rita Warren told me to stop apologizing, and I stopped. Immediately, my abilities began to ratchet upward. Eventually, I realized why: Trust is everything.

As my friend Bruce Moen says, "trust is always the issue" when exploring new abilities. Trust keeps the information flowing from Upstairs (higher self) to Downstairs (conscious self). Distrust impedes the flow.

Before knowledge, comes trust. Trust doesn't mean cocksure certainty. Rather, it is a halfway state between knowledge and ignorance. Belief and doubt, far from being opposites, are more or less the same thing, with a slightly different emphasis. Before you *know*, you *believe*, and belief is trust. But before you know, you also *doubt*, and doubt is distrust.

Operating from belief, rather than from knowledge, is in effect operating from a state of mingled trust and distrust. Is it any wonder that such efforts get mixed, uncertain results? Yet until we know, belief may be the best we can do. So where's the way out? How do we move from belief/doubt (which inhibits our efforts) to knowledge (which can only come from the experience that belief/doubt is preventing us from achieving)?

Here, my friends, we can only step into slightly deeper waters. "Believe, so that you may understand," one of the early fathers of the Christian church said. That admonition makes sense in this context. Belief, even though it implies doubt, may be the best we can do in the absence of knowledge. Sometimes, you have to operate from belief rather than knowledge until experience tells you what's what. That's what this whole book is about.

When I first became half-convinced that psychic abilities actually existed, I thought I would find them via the head. But I learned from experience that psychic ability—life—stems not from the head, but the heart. *Loving* is the key to life. Spiritual truths are proved by experience, and my talking about it won't convince you. Still, talking a little bit about it may make it seem respectable enough that you give it a try, so here goes.

I was 46 years old before I remembered what it was like to love. Before then, I thought I was loving enough. I fell in love, married, and had children. I loved my brothers and sisters and various relatives *from the state of being in which I lived.* But lower states of being cannot comprehend higher states. When we reach higher states, we look back at lower ones with compassion and pity. Now I see those years as largely wasted. So many opportunities to love; so little loving done. Instead, worries, ambitions, jealousies, anger, insecurities . . . .

It has been said that the ultimate polarity is between love and fear. This polarity could equally well be expressed as between hope (love) and despair (lack of love), or between openness and barriers. We live between these extremes, and we choose, day by day, which pole we move toward. If we are to live in health, if we are to help others heal, we must live in love as best we can from day to day.

The key to healing is to remove the illusion of separation, and the way to remove the illusion of separation is to love. It is the perception of separation that creates the perception of lack of control, which creates fear. Eliminate the perception of separation and fear goes out the window. This is what love does.

"Love" in this context is not about warm fuzzy feelings, or sentiment, or romance. We're talking about the binding energy, rather like gravity, that not only "makes the world go 'round,'" but *makes the world*. Love is the interpenetration of being, the fundamental oneness of everything. It is to life what flesh is to bodies. No love, no life.

Children in their natural state freely express love. ("Unless you become as little children," Jesus said, "you can't enter the kingdom.") As we age, we can become relatively dead to love, as we can be relatively dead to life itself, and for the same reason. Fortunately, once we know what's wrong, we can work to set it right. No matter where you are right now on the ability-to-love scale, you can teach yourself to love more deeply, more easily.

Here's a simple daily exercise to help you to practice love, extend your consciousness and your openness, and grow. It's not complicated or difficult. It just requires *doing*.

Find some object to love. It can be a pet or a flower or an abstraction or a car, though it would be better if it were a person. Do it! If you have difficulty doing it, go back in your mind to some time when you loved or felt loved.[1] Experience that feeling again; call it up, and express it toward whatever recipient you have chosen.

As you practice this, day by day, raise the bar by successively practicing loving something that's less lovable. Anyone can love a dog, because the dog

---

1 My thanks to Bruce Moen for this technique.

thinks you're wonderful. It takes a little more to love a cat, because the cat thinks *it's* wonderful. It takes more to love a woodchuck, because a woodchuck doesn't care one way or the other. It takes more to love a rattlesnake, because it's harder to relate to—especially if you're afraid of it. So you could easily raise the bar a little bit every day, just by aiming to love something that is continually a little bit less loveable.

It would be irresponsible to leave this subject without calling your attention to three dangers attendant to relying on intuition: psychic's disease, psychic inflation, and psychic self-delusion.

Psychic's Disease is what I call it when you confuse *strength* of feelings with *accuracy* of feelings. Just because you feel something strongly doesn't mean you're right. Just because you live relying on intuition doesn't mean that you shouldn't be checking that intuition against logic, common sense, and other people's judgment. Sometimes, intuition is right when logic, common sense, and other people's judgment are all wrong. Sometimes. Not always. Oliver Cromwell (of all people) was quoted as saying to those who were interpreting scripture, "I beseech you in the bowels of Christ, consider that you may be wrong." People with Psychic's Disease—and any of us may be afflicted with it, unpredictably, at any moment—never consider that they may be wrong. In my experience, those who think they are always right occasionally go *disastrously* wrong. It's only to be expected; they are trying to keep their balance without a gyroscope.

Psychic inflation is a well-known psychological phenomenon that can happen to people when they contact parts of reality that are larger than ordinary life. Some who begin to manifest psychic gifts have their lives enhanced. Others, in contact with the same manifestations, come to serious harm. The difference lies, at least in part, in whether they preserve their perspective and their humility.

A divine part of ourselves lives outside of time and space: This does not mean that we, in our ordinary Downstairs personality, should consider ourselves godly rather than mortal. We who are inside time and space need to remember that we are fallible; we are a part and not the whole. Inflation—identification with the divine *without remembering one's mortality*—leads not to further growth but to madness. It is, perhaps, the difference between Nietzsche and Carl Jung. The psychologist delved at least as deep as the philosopher, but Nietzsche seems to have fallen victim to inflation, and died mad, while Jung retained his dual perspective, and became ever wiser.

Psychic self-delusion, the third pitfall on the path of living in tune with intuition, is closely linked to psychic's disease. Just as those with psychic's disease over-value *opinion*, and consider certainty a guarantee of *accuracy*, so those with psychic self-delusion over-value *experience*, and consider certainty a guarantee of *reality*. Yes, so you had a given experience. Was it real? Was it necessarily what you took it to be? In any case, what does it mean? Don't be in too great a hurry to decide any of these questions. Second thoughts are cheap insurance against going too far off course.

Having said all that, it may be worth repeating: The way to obtain healing ability lies through trusting your internal knowledge, and working from an open heart. Although this course has its pitfalls, *all* courses have pitfalls. If we were to try to stay where we are until we find paths without perils, we would never move. The trick is to keep our eyes open as we move.

Chapter 7

Practices

Ultimately it comes to this. If you want health, you must work on yourself. If you want to be able to help others, you must work on yourself. If you want your life to move, rather than stagnate, you must work on yourself.

We heal ourselves—or others—less by what we *do* than by what we *are*. Before we turn to the question of helping others to heal, let's look at what we might do, on a regular basis, to raise our own resources—to work on ourselves. Everything we need do has already been stated or implied. It is a matter of building greater awareness of body, mind, emotion, and spirit; promoting internal communication among the four bodies; promoting greater day-to-day openness to "the other side," and, in short, leading lives that give our four bodies what they need.

1. Greater awareness

The materialist view of life leads to disconnection, illness, and death. It cannot do otherwise, because it overlooks or denies the greater part of what we are. Omit or deny the fact that part of us extends beyond time and space, and you confine yourself to dealing with the least powerful, least magical, part of us. What's more, you assure that you will not understand even the part that you do not deny.

The way to greater connection, then—the way to health— leads through ever-greater consciousness of the fact that we are body, mind, emotion, and spirit. Greater consciousness means more than merely assenting to the generalized proposition. It means feeling the truth of it; recognizing its manifestations in day-to-day life; and tracing out the various ways it manifests in our life. The more care we take to do that, the more powerful our connection to forces greater than our normal daily consciousness, and the less we will be swayed by unconscious fears, prejudices, and illnesses of body and spirit.

The "waters of life and health" meditation is one excellent way to get into touch. By paying attention to the pattern of the flow of the waters down your physical body, for example, you will get a better sense of what hurts, what is strained, what needs attention. Have you ever thought how little attention you give your body? I know I said it before, but it bears repeating.

A while ago, an energy worker asked me if I had ever hurt my right ankle. I started to say no—and then remembered that years earlier, while I was climbing a mountain in Peru, my foot had twisted and my ankle had hit the underlying rock so hard that at first I thought I had broken it. After six years, I had long forgotten the incident, but, as the energy worker quickly picked up, my body hadn't. Wouldn't it have been better for me to have remained conscious of that injury long enough to be sure it was really healed?

Similarly, emotions. Let a body worker start massaging your body and at some point you are very likely to see specific long-forgotten memories surface. It is not at all uncommon for massage therapists to see clients suddenly break into tears, without a word having been said. Some memories are painful, some aren't. What they have in common is that they were embedded in the flesh and are available to be released. You don't need to wait for the massage therapist.

Similarly, mental images, moods, prejudices, obsessions. Similarly (though perhaps not so specifically) blockages in the energy body. A little bit of attention on a regular basis prevents problems from stacking up.

2. Internal communication

Communication among the mental, emotional, energy, and physical bodies is as important to health as the well-being of any or all of them. It has been noted already that massage often will call forth memories and emotions by means of work in the physical, which suggests to me that it helps integrate the bodies. I suspect that psychoanalysis works better for those whose mental and emotional bodies are well connected than it does for those whose mental and emotional bodies have serious obstructions between them. And many energy workers have observed a connection between physical debility and breaks in the energy body.

Again, I gravitate toward the "waters of life and health" meditation, with the specific intent to erode whatever internal barriers impede communication among the bodies. I know this is a simple answer, but not every answer need be complicated. If the problem is that the bodies are communicating insufficiently, the solution is to remove whatever obstructs communication! There's no use making the solution more complicated than the problem.

3. Greater openness to "the other side"

Again, conceptually simple. The single most effective thing you need to do to achieve greater openness to the other side is—to *intend* it. The beginning of all my psychic development occurred some months after I (responding to an obscure prompting) took as my implicit prayer "greater openness to God, to my fellow man, and to all levels of myself."

In so doing, I did better than I knew. Looking at it later, I realized that this was the perfect prayer for psychic development. Openness to the greater reality beyond us (call it God, call it the underlying spiritual reality, call it All That Is); openness to all others, human and otherwise; openness to unsuspected aspects of ourselves.

I know nothing better to suggest. Phrase it any way you wish, but make a habit of affirming to yourself, every day, that you wish to achieve greater openness to God, to your fellow humans, and to all levels of yourself. I can't think of anything worthwhile that this doesn't cover.

4. Giving our four bodies what they need

This requirement is a little harder, not because the subject is unplowed ground but because our society downplays and denigrates so much of what is needed. To live our lives in a sensible way cuts against the grain of much of what our society values.

We should consider ourselves to be either one unit or a system of coordinated bodies. Which way you choose to see us depends on how you like to think of yourself. Either way, it is necessary to remember that the energetic, emotional, and mental bodies have their needs, too.

The needs of the physical body are pretty well understood at one level: nutrition, exercise, rest. It needs more than that, however. It needs loving attention and appreciation more systematically applied, so that we become consciously aware of its injuries, illnesses, and weaknesses. It needs our understanding of its connection to the part of itself that extends beyond time and space (its non-physical extensions) and to the other three bodies. Until you recognize that it extends beyond the physical, you will be unable to recognize or correct problems that have their roots in that shadow area. Likewise, if you don't understand the connection with the other three bodies, you often will look in the wrong place for the source of problems. But if you take good care of the physical, the energetic level likely will be taken care of at the same time, automatically.

The needs of the emotional and mental bodies, as understood by psychologists, include the ability to receive and process information from the world, and the ability to initiate and evaluate action that will affect the world. Abraham Maslow devised a hierarchy of needs that begins with the most elementary physical requirements and ends with self-actualization. It all implies that we need nurturance, stability, and challenge, in small enough doses that we can deal with them successfully, and large enough to aid our growth. Of course, we can't specify how much anyone needs of any or all. One man's meat is another man's poison.

Research on prayer and its impact on groups with illnesses shows that it has a powerful benign effect. Have you ever wondered why?

5. Helping others

When people work together in love, intending to help one another, they implicitly destroy the illusion that there is distance between people, and this provides a supportive field that helps the person to heal. The practice of love is the practice of overcoming the illusion of distance, and prayer is the practice of love.

Now, this isn't the way that people usually think about prayer. In fact, many people probably would strongly object to this characterization of what they're doing. They may think they are praying to a God who can say, "Well, yes, I think I'll grant your prayer," or, "No, no, you're not really worthy." It doesn't matter. When people sincerely pray, they love without thought for themselves, and this has a powerful effect, regardless what opinion they may have about what they are doing or why they are doing it. An old cliché says, "Prayer doesn't change things, prayer changes people and people change things." Whoever coined that saying meant it in a different way, but this meaning is true as well.

6. Hands-on healing

Religious tradition over uncounted thousands of years maintains that we can help each other to heal. Healing always proceeds from love, and it always depends upon the fact that at another level we are one with the source of life—and hence are one with each other. Here in the world of duality we experience ourselves and each other as separate and distinct. But the part of ourselves that extends beyond time and space—the part of ourselves often called spirit—is part of a very different reality, subject to fewer rules because not subject to the illusion of separation or the law of delayed consequences.

To put it into terms Christians would recognize (though perhaps only in shock, in this context), the disciples of Jesus learned to heal others not by their own power but by the power Jesus connected them to. "Not me, but Christ in me." We might paraphrase it this way: "My personal power, brought up to a higher power, and brought down again to the other person." We as Downstairs individuals focus the power and sometimes help direct it. We do not originate it. And we don't need to prove that this higher power is part of us or separate from us. There's no use getting lost in definitions. Just know that the power exists, and that we can tap into it. E.F. Schumacher used to say, "It's amazing how much theory we can dispense with, once we set out to do some real work."

Helping others to connect to the healing source is simple. The difficulty is to be sure of your motivations and of their situation. Are you trying to help—to be a channel of blessings—or are you seeking thrills or glory? Are you helping them, or interfering? Because, again, remember, illness often serves an important purpose. That's why you ask permission of the person, or of the person's Upstairs component, before attempting to heal, to be sure that they are done with the illness before you remove it.

Within those restrictions, it really is that simple. Remember that you are far more than your physical body and more than your Downstairs personality. Remember always to come from a place of love, seeking only to assist. All the healing techniques that have been invented, some of them quite complicated, can do no more than this. This is not to say that these other techniques are not necessary for some people, but the reason why they are necessary is because they function as belief crutches. For some people, the need for crutches is short-lived. Others rely on them for their whole lives. There's nothing wrong with using crutches if you think you need them. Just remember, Jesus was not a Reiki master.

Remember, too, that you aren't sending energy, though that's what it feels like. When you're doing hands-on healing, you often have the sense of energy flowing through you—especially through your hands—into the person. There's no harm in thinking of it that way, but it may be that this isn't really what you're doing. Maybe you are resonating at a state of health, rather like a tuning fork, so that the other person can "lean on" that resonance in order to retune.

What is important is not the mechanism but the intent. You *intend* that help should be given and help should be received. You lower the internal barriers that would prevent the flow. That's all there is to it. Sometimes you perceive the transfer as a tingling, sometimes as heat, sometimes as a transfer of energy, sometimes as prickles. The experience is more a function of your concepts and expectations than it is of what's really happening. That's one reason why different people use entirely different concepts yet both get good results. Neither way of doing things is invalid. Neither one is "just imagination." Each one is just the result of the person's state of being.

By the way, this is also why some people are able to experience miracles, and some only gradual healing, and others no healing at all. The difference is not in the seriousness of the illness, or in the ability of the person conducting the healing. Mostly, it is in the mental structure of the person on the receiving end. How much can s/he experience? A good Catholic at Lourdes, say, if fully prepared to experience a miracle, may or may not experience it—but at any rate probably will not have internal mental or spiritual barriers (unconscious expectations) that would make miracles impossible. Healings manifest according to the limitations of a person's belief systems.

7. Distant healing

After you accept the idea of hands-on healing, the next step is what is called distant healing. For some, this is one concept too far: They can't bring themselves to believe that such a thing is possible. Yet it is no step at all. The only difference between hands-on healing and healing at a distance is—distance. But this isn't the obstacle that it first appears.

We in bodies live in time and space, of course, but our minds and bodies extend *beyond* time and space. By definition, there can be no separation by space where there is no space, and no separation by time where there is no time. Although the part of us that is in space-time experiences separation, the part of us that isn't, doesn't. Thus part of us lives in a "space" with different rules and fewer boundaries. When we connect with that part of ourselves, miracles happen.

When you know that there is no distance to be overcome, you realize that distant healing is not a matter of overcoming distance, but of overcoming *the idea* of overcoming distance. Surely it's a lot easier to overcome an idea than a physical "reality." Healing, whether hands-on or at a distance, is the

same thing. You hold yourself at a level of health and resonate with the person needing healing, and s/he revs up to that
level, as if leaning upon the template of health that you are
holding.

Part Four

WHAT CAN
BE DONE

Chapter 8

Dealing with Myself

I said in the introduction to this book that I can't promise perfect health any more than I could promise a life without problems. That's not what life seems to be about. Instead, I am offering you another way to look at your health, and your life, that takes you out of helpless victim mode and reminds you that you are in charge.

Thinking that I would provide a few examples from my own life, I went through eight years of my journals, using health-related entries to remind myself of what I had been up against and what I had learned. I then sorted the material into two categories: conditions and remedies. The problems range from serious (asthma and heart-related problems) to trivial (cuts and burns) but they do demonstrate how broad a range of problems we are able to address on our own, or with friends. Before we look at them, a few words about a couple of aspects of healing that don't always receive enough attention.

In December, 2005, as I was working on this book, I found myself struggling against a persistent bout of sickness—while writing about wellness! A friend (bless him) asked me if I had asked my friends Upstairs what was going on. They said, simply, "Well what do you need to know? You are writing on healing, it is as well to remember what it *really* is like to be sick and be unable to talk it away."

Instant revelation! That is so true! Sometimes well-meaning folks say to sick friends, "You can be well if you wish." This is true in the largest sense, but to the sick it sounds like they are being told: "If you are sick, it's your own fault." Try being on the receiving end of that advice and see if it helps. Yes, our health is under our own control—but not necessarily under our *conscious* control. In fact, I would argue that by definition we get sick for reasons *beyond* our conscious control. Other layers of consciousness introduce or allow illness, for reasons that seem good and sufficient to them.

Well, obviously, if an illness is caused *unconsciously*, we can't just *talk* it away, or *wish* it away. We have to find the key—and that means we have to bring the cause to consciousness and deal with it. *That's all we're doing here.* Every technique that I suggest here amounts to one more way to move a health problem from the realm of the unconscious (where we cannot much affect it) to the realm of consciousness, where we can make whatever change is needed.

However, some discretion is advisable.

When I first discovered that I could transmit healing energies, I was elated, and fell prey to a very common pitfall among well-meaning new healers. Being excited by a sense of new possibilities, I jumped to the unconscious conclusion that I could and should heal anything and anyone. This amounted to assuming that illness is by definition bad, and that removing the illness is by definition good. This delusion leads to what is called "the healer out of control."

Like most delusions, this one is cured by time and reflection. I had four friends. One was a very sick, elderly lady; another, a younger woman with breast cancer; a third, a man my age with a brain tumor; a fourth, an older man with multiple injuries following a car crash. I—and others—did healing work on Meredith, on Joyce, on Dave, and on Martin. In each case, I felt the energy go forth, and felt that it was received. *But they all died.*

For a long while I considered these to be efforts that had inexplicably failed. It was only after some time that I realized that sometimes the healing a person needs is release from life. Sometimes healing energy is the energy that enables a person to make a good transition. It was good to learn that, and especially it was good to learn that it is a mistake to be attached to outcomes.

It is always good to offer love and healing energy, but the outcome is not up to us. Nor are we necessarily competent to judge that outcome. What looks tragic to us may in fact (viewed from inside that life, or from an Upstairs perspective) be triumph. To really know, we would have to be competent to judge the entire pattern of someone else's life. We can never know, and we don't need to know, and don't necessarily have a right to know.

Another thing. We really ought to stop thinking of illness as an enemy, and start thinking of it instead as a messenger. I would make a small bet that you know more than one person who has come down with an illness, been cured of it—perhaps miraculously—and had it recur. Perhaps they have gone through the cycle more than once. But unless and until we make real changes in response to an illness, that is naturally what's going to happen. Illness isn't an irrelevant interruption of our lives, and healing isn't necessarily a return to the life we were leading before the illness "interrupted" it.

A few years ago I had dinner with a man who three years previously had been dying of AIDS and now was well. What was his secret? Simply this. Rather than fight the illness or regard it as something that had inexplicably entered his life as an invader, he fully accepted it as a message from life itself. He accepted it as something that was part of the pattern of this life, something that *had a right to be there*. Taking this idea seriously, he examined his life, made the changes the disease suggested, and at some point, apparently, the disease was no longer needed, and went away.

Conditions

All right, let's move on to specifics. Here is a list of a few of the conditions I deal with in my life, followed by a list of some of the tools that have helped. I know this it is "all about me," and I apologize, but this is what I know first-hand. I put it here assuming that you will read it with an eye toward finding whatever may be here for you.

1. Asthma

In terms of impact and seriousness, and sheer duration, asthma takes pride of place. Because of my attitude toward the medical system, I had a hard time getting asthma under control. I am prone to assume that mental and spiritual powers are everything. I have had to learn that the causes of my sickness may be physical as well as mental. After far too long, I have learned what would have been obvious to others, that those physical causes may be alleviated by life changes such as attention to diet, moderate exercise, and clarification of my emotional life. Beyond that, I have tried various things. Some of the energy techniques listed below often help, too, especially the control panel. But, as long as the condition recurs, I have to assume that things in my life still require correction.

2. Eye problems

Next in importance after my lungs and heart, in terms of worrying me, are my eyes, for three reasons. First, I was diagnosed as having *borderline glaucoma* more than thirty years ago. I wouldn't take the prescription drugs that the medical establishment prefers, because the side effects are not trivial, and conventional medicine has little else to offer.

Second, in 1998, and then again a few years later, and occasionally since, I have experienced a strange condition I call *The Dazzle*. It is a dazzling light shaped like an irregular ring, around the center of my eye. Where does the light come from? Why? And why does it go? I don't have a clue. The Dazzle has made me unable to read, nearly unable to see, for minutes at a time, once as long as an hour. (For all I know, it may be connected to the borderline glaucoma.)

And third, there's simple *eyestrain*. I read too much, and I stay on the computer too long. Sometimes I awaken with a headache, eyes hurting. Each time, I remind myself that this is pretty dumb, and for a while I am more careful. I suppose everybody overworks their eyes from time to time, and I don't think I'd pay too much attention if it weren't for the specter of glaucoma lurking in the background, and The Dazzle. None-theless it is a concern.

Below when I talk about the control panel, I describe the only way I know how to deal with these three eye conditions.

3. Blood sugar

Speaking of lifestyle! I am prone to overeating, particularly at night. It is always humiliating to realize how dependent I am on continuous inputs of food that I don't need. Peri-odically I make efforts to reform, which succeed for a while and are again forgotten. For years, every so often, the Guys Upstairs have put me on notice that I simply *must* live more sensibly, or suffer consequences. They said, once, "You *can't* fool with your blood sugar as you did yesterday—half a bag of chocolate chip cookies—without consequences. You *must* see that by now. Mind is not everything in that respect. Your body is crystallized visualization, you could say, and should be molded, not shattered or stressed."

Another time, I woke up to a headache and a constricted feeling in the tissues of my whole upper trunk (hard to describe), and a knowing that might as well have been a voice, saying, "You're going to get diabetes if you don't change your ways *now*." The suggested change was simple enough: Much more salad greens, fewer sweets and breads—mostly no bread or sweets late at night. (I found that odd. Why should it mat-ter *when* one eats something? But that's what I heard.)

Yet another time, I asked why I was napping, and why I woke up aching, and they said, "Your life could use more exercise to prevent your metabolism from becoming ever more sluggish. And your consumption of pancakes and molasses—though more moderate than heretofore—was still enough to kick you over into sleep, as that big piece of chocolate cake was, the other day."

Slowly, over time, I have been listening, and moderating. I read of someone who learned to ask the body what it really wanted, as opposed to what we assumed that it wanted, from habit and what we might call manufactured appetite. I do that, when I remember to do it, and when I am not deafened by an internal clamoring for something like bread or potatoes. But nothing ever really helped much except periodic fasting—which addresses the result (overweight) but not the cause (incorrect eating habits)—and resetting my control panel, as I will describe below.

4. Heart problems

Several years ago, I suffered apparent congestive heart failure, which was corrected by distant healing from the nine-year-old daughter of a friend! Karis' magic seems to have restored my heart to health. Judging by symptoms (and I don't know how else to judge), things are normal. I am strong, I have endurance, I don't experience chest pains. So far, so good, I would say.

5. Etcetera

Beyond these problems I have the usual irritations we all have. Nothing really worth mentioning, because none is life-threatening or even particularly serious. So let us turn to an examination of various remedies I have found, some of which you may wish to explore.

Here I list the things that have helped me, listing only those things of which I have personal experience. What I omit (conscious breathing, for instance) may easily be of equal or greater importance to you. Finding them is your business. Take this as a reminder to search.

1. Access Upstairs

I'd put this one first and foremost. A mighty big advantage. For instance, I have had to learn to overcome depression of spirit. The easiest, most effective way to do it is to remember that we are more than our physical bodies—and the way to keep that real to ourselves is to maintain access Upstairs. In the midst of my congestive heart failure incident, when I asked The Gentlemen Upstairs if the problem didn't "make a mockery of access and expanded perception and such-like," they replied that a short experience of difficulty *grounds* what we think we know. Battles and struggles and suffering, they said, serve to *ground* who we are, at a deeper level.

"Struggle brings forth potential and manifests it. That is what grounding *is*." See Chapter Ten for various techniques that will help you maintain access.

2. Attention

I have found that I can help my body readjust itself simply by paying attention to it. For instance, sometimes, when I remember to, I scan my body before rising. If I find this or that muscle aching. I move my attention to that place and it changes, it adjusts, apparently just because I have my attention on it. This "working from the inside"—though too simple to say, almost—really has the core of something important.

3. Awareness hands (a tool of visualization)

Visualizing your energy body as a copy of your physical body, use that body's "awareness hands." Try using them to massage some part of the body that aches. I sometimes use them in the third eye area, trying to stimulate mental or psychic activity. Think of them as a way of visualizing exactly the result you want. In other words, if you want a given muscle to relax, visualize your energy hands, your awareness hands, smoothing it out. Experiment!

4. Control panel (a tool of visualization)

This is a *big* one, for me. I first heard of the concept at a conference. Someone asked legendary psychic Ingo Swann how we go about changing things we wanted to change about ourselves. "Just go to your control panel," he said in essence, "and change it." In other words, visualize a control panel; visualize a particular control within it, and move it to whatever setting you want it to be at. This simple, elegant visualization gives you an effective visual way to convey your desires to your unconscious mind. Whatever you want to change, try changing it from the control panel. If you have a physical problem, visualize the switch for that problem and move it. Set it to zero if you can. If you can't, get it lower anyway, and repeatedly go back to lower it more. Monitor your life, lest massive changes happen and you not even notice! It should (but doesn't) go without saying that if you want results, it is well for you not to make one choice via the control panel and then make a contradictory choice in your life decisions. You have to mean it.

(Does this sound too easy? All I can say is, try it. It's your life, and you get to choose from within whatever situation you find yourself in. It is true, the situation may be set up at birth, and may change seemingly in response to external events. Your mental, emotional, and physical filters may obstruct response to your changing pre-set positions. But this is one of those cases where perseverance is all. Determine what you want to be, and continually, consistently make the same choices, and you will get there.)

5. Diet

Intuitive as I am (that is, not much inclined toward sensory evidence) it took me a long time to give diet its proper importance. I always inclined to believe that we ought to be able to transmute pretty much anything to our body's use. Actually, I still do believe that. The only thing is, diet is an easy way of removing obstacles on the body end of the body-mind polarity that determines our health. I didn't used to understand this. As one example, I substituted coconut milk for cow's milk, and my health improved markedly. I still eat cheese and other dairy products, but the elimination of cow's milk has made a big difference. You may find that some experimentation in diet pays big dividends. (Just don't go off the deep end. We weren't created to be slaves to fad diets.)

6. Ear-candling

Now, here's one that really sounds wacko, yet works. You need to find someone who knows what they're doing. The practitioner positions, at the edge of your ear canal, a funnel made of beeswax, *and sets it on fire!* The heat of the fire melts hardened ear wax and draws it up where it deposits on the funnel. Sounds crazy as hell, but it works like a charm.

7. Exercise

I admit it, I'm not much for exercise. Walking and canoeing are about the only forms of exercise I thoroughly approve of. Nonetheless, it is obvious that these bodies were made to be used, and function best when they receive the kind of maintenance provided, for example, by the lymph system, which exercise assists. Do as I say, not as I do.

8. Fasting

The first time that I heard my brother describing the benefits he derived from occasional fasting, perhaps twenty-five years ago, something went "click" and I knew I'd have to try that. Sometimes I fasted looking for mental clarity, other times for weight loss, usually for both. Both these results I usually got, but in both cases the results are fleeting unless backed up by a change in physical or mental life-style. And that's about what would be expected, is it not? Nonetheless, as a method of interrupting your "regular" life to help you gain perspective, fasting is first rate.

9. Medical massage

This is a powerful tool, removing problems from the physical end of the mind-body connection. Find a really good medical massage therapist. We're not talking about relaxation here, but correction of physical problems that express—and contribute to—mental and emotional problems. This has been perhaps the most important non-emergency professional technique I have benefited from.

10. Meditation

I hope I have said enough about mediation by this point to convince you of its uses. Although I primarily use *The Waters of Life and Health* meditation to clear physical and energetic blockages, it occurred to me one day to try it as a way of clearing the sources of emotional problems with others. You might try that.

11. Resonant energy balloon (a tool of visualization)

This is one of those infinitely useful Monroe Institute tools that harness the conscious mind with the subconscious. Visualize yourself creating a balloon of energy around yourself, and give it whatever properties you prefer. *It is a tool of visualization*, and so you might think of it as a way to manifest magic (via the subconscious mind). I once suggested to an allergy-ridden friend that she pop a continuing resonant energy balloon (rebal) against the ill effects of any food. What is it, after all, but a comprehensible sign to the subconscious mind to be on the alert? Experiment.

12. Rest

Wouldn't you think that the need for rest would be too evident to people to need mention? Perhaps, if someone could find a way to make money on it, it would be advertised instead of patent-medicines. When I get sick (assuming it is not asthma, which makes obtaining rest almost impossible) my preferred remedy is not medicine but water, warmth, and rest. In other words, I drink water and go to bed and try to stay there till my body recovers. If you've never tried this, you may be amazed how well it works, and how surely.

13. *Ritual*

Ritual can be used to recollect us to ourselves. For example, here is a simple ritual that could change your life. Breathe, consciously, five minutes a day or so, at a fixed time. Another example. Trying to get a handle on eating more consciously? Create a ritual—perhaps merely saying a grace—before eating.

14. *Water*

Like rest, simple and easy to overlook, because nobody is making any money on it. I'm not talking about bottled water. Buy a filtering device, filter your water and keep it in the refrigerator and drink from it, rather than from the tap, unless you are in a rural area with good water. Most of our body is water. Water smoothes all bodily functions. It helps process toxins released by exercise, it helps you ground new states of being, and it just generally assists the body to function smoothly. You can't buy anything to equal it.

15. *Vitamins and minerals*

A friend who is an ENT doctor told me that most of his asthmatic patients are low on magnesium and D3. Ever since he told me that, I have made a point of taking one of each in the morning, and it does seem to help. You may find that your body needs more of a certain vitamin or mineral than it gets naturally. Consider being tested for those needs. Not a magic bullet, but it's always worthwhile to remember to work from both ends of the body-mind connection.

16. *Yoga*

We often store negativity in the body, hiding it from the mind, or rather averting our gaze. But negative energy is a fact of life like positive energy. You can't have one without having both. The trick is to bring yourself into balance, recognizing that light and dark are both part of one whole. Instead of trying to make reality one-sided, which it can never be, instead of denying or rejecting the negative, absorb and release it. Yoga is a good way to learn to do this.

You *can* call spirits from the vasty deep—and they *will* come when you do call them. The next chapter will give some examples of things I've seen firsthand.

Chapter 9

Dealing with Others

The three most important variables in healing are:

1. The healer's faith/confidence in what is possible

2. The openness (or otherwise) of the "healee" to different treatments

3. The faith or confidence of the "healee" in the healer

The variables are going to differ according to the nature of the problem, but that doesn't mean that different people are going to react the same way to the same problems. What is easy for some is impossible for others, and what is impossible one day perhaps becomes conceivable the next, doable the day after that, and routine shortly thereafter.

You might think that some things would be obviously beyond the reach of energy medicine. Brain surgery, for instance. Setting broken bones. Kidney dialysis. MS, or Parkinson's, or diabetes. Certainly it would be foolhardy—criminally foolhardy—for a healer to encourage someone with such a condition to bypass the established medical system, regardless of the system's defects. But that doesn't mean that energy medicine is necessarily helpless even in the face of such conditions. If healers can cure cancer, remove tumors, rebuild the immune system, rebalance the body's endocrine system, etc., etc., it seems to me extremely unsafe to say flatly that this or that is beyond their reach.

I, myself, find it impossible to conceive of re-setting a broken bone, or straightening a bone that healed crooked, using only such techniques as I have. Therefore, for me it is impossible. Whether it would be impossible for others, I don't know. But everything else on the list above it seems to me falls within the competence of the body's own regulatory mechanisms, all of which are under the control of our subconscious mind. I can't really say that anything is impossible. So much depends on the would-be healer's beliefs.

And just as much depends on the "healee." When I was still very new to this, I occasionally worked, or tried to work, on people whose skepticism amounted to almost a vested interest in proving that no help could come from this direction. Naturally, their closed-off nature assured that they would be right. It took only a few such experiences for me to realize that an essential was that the healee not be closed to the possibility. They don't have to *believe*, so long as they have not committed themselves to actively *disbelieve*. In most cases, the first time they feel the energy or perceive improvement, their belief system evolves pretty rapidly!

What's "the best method" of healing? Whatever works. Some people believe in one technique, and they stick to it.

Nothing wrong with that. But since I do as I am led, I wind up doing one thing one time and something else another time. As long as it works, that's all I ask. I'm perfectly happy to follow intuition, making it up as I go along.

In eight years of journal notes I found more than 115 mentions of healing work—mostly mere mentions, without details. Among the things I mentioned working on were: ankle swelling; pain in walking; bunched muscles of ankle and leg or of the upper arm; cancer in the lymph cells of throat and groin; circulation of hands and feet; cough caused by tension; balancing energy, or boosting energy; fatigue, insomnia; "feeling vague, not quite there"; problems hearing; knee pain following injury; laryngitis; muscular pain in hands, back, neck, or shoulder; persistent nosebleeds; pulled thigh muscle; realigning mental and emotional bodies; restricted movement in feet; sinus headache; sinus trouble; sore throat; swollen ankle following injury; throat, ear, and sinus problem (connected); chest problem; TMJ.

That's quite a mixed bag, but not particularly anything special. Many people have done far more than I, but these things I can attest to, because I was there. These are not second-hand miracle stories, but first-hand accounts that perhaps will give you a wider sense of the possible. So, without trying to come up with definite lines of demarcation, here are a few of the healings that I have participated in.

It seems easiest to put the conditions in alphabetical order.

Bell's Palsy

A friend in Great Britain asked if we could help his wife, who had suffered an attack of Bell's Palsy. A friend and I worked together for about half an hour one night, going into a very deep meditation, trying to help. This turned out to be a very strong experience. I "clicked out" (Monroe-speak for functioning for a while and bringing back no memory of it) and returned to normal consciousness freezing cold—always a good sign of contact, for me—and with a very sore neck. (I was sitting in a rocking chair and my head had slumped sideways.) I called the next morning to see if she had noticed any change. (I would have been astonished if she had not, the energy flow was so strong.) She awoke without the headache that had accompanied the palsy for a month, and later reported that she was "zinging with energy." Three years on, the pain and fatigue had not returned.

Burns

As I was at the cash register waiting to pay for breakfast, I saw that the waitress was grasping ice with her right hand. She explained that she had picked up a plate that was too hot and had burned her four fingertips and thumb, which I could see were an angry red. I somewhat hesitantly asked if she would be open to a little energy work, and she was, though she didn't know what I was going to do. She flinched as I reached toward her hand, thinking I was going to touch her fingers. Instead I put one hand beneath hers, steadying it, and using my left hand to sort of stroke the energy of the burn away. She must have been very open to it, because in seconds she said, "The throbbing has stopped!" I had to leave—my friends were already in the car waiting—so I showed her how to do it for herself, and hoped for the best. I expect that after a few minutes the throbbing returned and she had to use more ice (which would be a good idea in any case). But she now knows that she isn't as helpless as she had thought.

Cuts

I was sitting at a table in a restaurant with a family I knew and the father mentioned that he had cut his hand, and it was bothering him. Automatically, I reached out and sent energy. I knew it had worked when he suddenly turned to me, his eye wide and incredulous. On another day, I did the same for his daughter's ankle, that I had done for her father's hand, and in a few seconds she said it was fine.

Diagnosis, long distance

A friend called from across the country. Why was he so sick? Why did his back hurt? As we talked, I sensed he had a lower back injury at the reverse curve, and it turned out that indeed he did. He was used to seeing a chiropractor to treat this long-term problem, but hadn't lately. I also got the words "opportunistic infection," as the source of his illness, which also fit. Finally (he had been going through very hard times at home and at work), we smoothed his emotional and mental bodies—his emotional body felt quite dull around the heart. Bear in mind that he, too, was very experienced in meditation, visualization, and healing, and so presented no obstacles.

Dislocation, long-term effects

One night a friend told me that for more than twenty years she had had discomfort and limitations of mobility in her right arm and shoulder as a result of a shoulder dislocation. Chiropractors could always get the shoulder back in position, but could never get it to stay. So she had learned to make certain movements only in a certain way, to avoid a catch in her motion. As she was telling me this I was wondering in some dismay how I could help. I had no idea how to approach the problem. But it turned out that she wasn't asking for help, she was leading up to telling me that about a month ago she'd noticed that the impairment seemingly no longer existed! We had never worked on it or even thought about it, so far as either of us could remember. The closest thing we could think of was my working with her and directing that the energy fix "anything that needs fixing," though not in those words probably. That was quite a moment!

Emphysema

The sister of one of my friends has emphysema but still smokes. Naturally the combination is pretty debilitating. We had only a limited time together, so I concentrated on teaching her how to visualize her way to energy assistance using the "waters of life and health" meditation. It didn't take her long to feel the difference. For one thing, her chronic cough departed (temporarily). I never found out if she built on this or lost it. Of course, the final result for her, as for everyone, would be up to her.

Eyes

Eyes are a big deal! Where would we be without them? I remember, particularly, two kinds of eye conditions I have worked on.

The first was one of my employees, a young woman who suffered from dry eye. A little energy work got it to be temporarily normal, and I showed her how to maintain it that way using visualization. This was new to her belief system, so I was not surprised that in the course of one afternoon she went from normal, to teary, to dry, several times. She had learned to do it, but hadn't learned to keep it from fluctuating as her belief fluctuated. She left our employ shortly thereafter, so I never did find out if she made the change permanent, or relapsed into helplessness. Unless she learned (*really* learned) that physical ailments are connected with the rest of our lives, I would guess the latter.

The second—perhaps the most satisfying bit of healing I have ever done—involved an 83-year-old friend. For twenty years she had suffered from blurry vision in her right eye, following lens replacements in two cataract operations. The right eye never focused as it should. When she told me that, I said, "We ought to be able to do something about that," and while I provided the usual energy boost, I talked her through a visualization of the eye muscle lengthening or shortening until it reached the proper focal distance. Well, my friend is very experienced in energy work: It didn't take us five minutes –after twenty years! The correction slipped once, and we corrected it again. After that, it proved to be permanent.

Gall stone

One of the most interesting and startling early efforts involved removing a gall stone without surgery. A friend had had this stone for years. Whenever she leaned back against a chair she could feel it. It had never gotten painful enough for surgery, but it was uncomfortable. When she mentioned it, I suggested that we visualize the stone gone—that is, envision the gall bladder normal, without stones. This we did, and—although

I realize full well that this is going to stress your belief system—the stone did indeed disappear. At least, she never felt it again, which is all she cared about.

Headache

Removing or alleviating headaches often astonishes people, and those who suffer from migraines, in particular, are incredulous and wonderfully grateful. I notice that with different people I am led to use different techniques. Sometimes I lightly massage the sides of their heads while talking to them, sometimes I have them visualize the headache exiting through the crown of their head, sometimes I put the palms of my hands against their temples and gently rock up and down. Like so much of this work, it's easy to do, hard to describe.

Pain

This isn't a scientific way of categorizing things, so perhaps I may be excused for lumping several kinds of things simply under the category of "removing pain." Now, in talking about "removing pain," it is important to remember that the function of pain is to warn us that something is wrong. We often use a sort of verbal shorthand, saying we want to remove the pain when what we really mean is that we want to remove the pain *and the cause of the pain.* Nothing wrong with that, as long as we're clear about our intention. But to remove the pain without removing the condition the pain is warning us against would be worse than useless, and could be dangerous. What sense does it make to treat symptoms and leave causes untreated and undetected?

Some pain follows operations, or injuries such as cuts or burns. In those cases, I see no reason to hesitate to take it away. The healing is going on automatically; the notification that the pain provides is not needed. It's usually easy enough to remove. Sometimes we experience muscle pain seemingly without reason. In such cases, I specify, as I talk to the person, that we want muscles to return to their normal condition. In other words, we want to remove the *cause* of the pain, not just the pain itself. And sometimes we experience long-term pain from an unresolved injury. For instance, my sister slipped on a step and banged her shin in 1960, and in forty years it never healed! It ached in cold weather, it was sore to the touch. I only learned about it a few years ago. When I did, it wasn't that hard, using energy work and careful massage around it (not over it), to bring the area back to normal. Think of that. Forty years of pain, when it could have been avoided if someone had taught her how to overcome the reason for it.

Restoring mobility

A friend visited my office, unable to raise her right elbow to the level of her shoulders. She left with full mobility. What was the magic? A little work on the muscles, a little energy work, active visualization on her part, guided by my narrative.

Shingles

Two of my friends, each a generation older than me, have suffered from shingles, which I gather is supposed to be incurable. Both friends were very open to energy work, and skilled in visualization. For one, it took two sessions; for the other, a couple more. But in both cases—using energy techniques only, no medicines, no expensive (or inexpensive) procedures—we got the pain to leave and stay gone.

Shoulder and neck injury

After a friend injured her shoulder and neck in a fall, for months she couldn't move her neck freely. Her doctor was able to loosen up the muscles using hot packs, but was unable to provide permanent assistance. I could provide temporary and superficial relief through massaging the affected muscles, but we did not make any dramatic progress until one day she began using her "awareness hands" (as described in Chapter Seven) to work from the inside, while I worked on the outside. We had a particular advantage in that she was a massage therapist—which means she had expert knowledge of the location and functioning of the muscles involved—and was very experienced in visualization and in energy work.

Plants

It may not be out of place here to mention that I have found that plants are exceptionally responsive to love and admiration. It is more than a matter of physical care. Perhaps this is the secret of some people's green thumb, and other people's "black thumb."

Reading this, you might get the impression that healing work is a major part of my day-to-day life. It isn't. Mostly it happens between the lines, and none of it takes very long. But in terms of importance, it is. I jump at whatever opportunities arise, for there isn't anything that I find more satisfying, especially when two or three of us are working together. But it isn't something for only a chosen few. It is life as I have learned to lead it, as you can learn to lead it. I would be very pleased if these stories encourage you to learn how much more you can do for yourself and for others.

Chapter 10

You Can Do This!

The main text contains or implies everything I know about taking charge of your health. But perhaps it is worthwhile to spell it out a little, if only to provide an even quicker reference. So here it is.

Working from the assumption that the pattern of your health is part of the pattern of your life, doesn't it follow that you should put some attention to how you live? If you live a balanced, sane, connected life, you have reason to expect better health than if you live in an unbalanced insane, disconnected way. Just as figs don't grow from thistles, no part of our life is *really* disconnected from all other parts of our life, no matter how it may appear. That being said, perhaps your life *is* unbalanced, insane, disconnected, at least in part, and you haven't yet found a way to fix what is out of control You don't have to wait to correct your circumstances to counter their effect on you.

First, let's define our goal. It seems to me that whether we are talking about health or about life, usually we are using one or more of five verbs: Change, Repair, Improve, Maintain,

Protect. Conveniently enough, they provide a neat acronym: CRIMP. Nothing crimps life like bad health, and nothing crimps health like bad living, so why put up with it either way?

Change, Repair, Improve, Maintain, Protect. The first three imply alteration, and the final two imply holding on to what is. So do we have five verbs, or two conditions? Both. Neither. For our purposes, we have five special cases of two conditions that boil down to attaining and maintaining greater control of our life and health. No more, no less. It isn't complicated.

These simple techniques to help you live your life amount to (1) staying connected, and (2) directing your life.

Staying Connected

First, you want to stay *connected*. Especially amid the stress of ordinary life, and of crises within ordinary life, staying connected is your ace in the hole. And it isn't hard to do, in itself. What is hard is that it requires that you remember to actually *do* it. Here are four variations on the same theme:

1. If you can *pray*, pray, routinely, matter-of-factly, with faith that your prayer is heard. Don't just ask for change, but be grateful for what you have. Don't think of yourself as a worm of a sinner, unworthy to be heard, but think of yourself as co-creator of your life. Don't beg; confidently expect. Don't whine; seek to understand. You are not alone, regardless how it sometimes feels.

2. If you can't pray (or even if you can), *meditate*. Quiet the mind and feel yourself a part of all of life. If trying to dismiss

all thought leads only to distractions and wool-gathering, try holding your mind to one image, one idea, something like, "I am part of all life, visible and invisible, and I will not be led out into the wilderness and abandoned there." Meditation lessens your fear and your sense of isolation, and if it did nothing else, it would be well worthwhile.

3. If you can't pray or meditate (or even if you can), you can always *visualize*. Now, *this does not mean seeing pictures!* It isn't like you close your eyes and a movie starts showing. *Visualizing* is *imagining*. You do it every time you remember something past, or daydream about something you're looking forward to. Visualizing is holding in your mind an image, or an idea, or a feeling. Everybody on earth does it. Don't be misled by the connotations of the word. I'll spell out a few useful visualizations below.

4. Finally, if you can't pray or meditate or visualize (or even if you can), you can always *relax*. Sitting quietly, or lying down—comfortable enough to relax, but not so comfortable as to fall asleep—close your eyes. Sometimes you can hear your pulse, thumping in your ears. Even if you can't, you can always concentrate on your breathing. In either case, first fall into the rhythm and then consciously, calmly, imagine it slowing down. Yes, you can affect your heartbeat, just as you can affect your breathing. Slow it down, and just for a few minutes calmly relax. You do have the right to relax! Anything that is stressing you will still be there when you finish, but for these few minutes this is *your* time. Relax. Then develop the

habit of reminding yourself, in your normal world, to every so often remember what relaxation feels like.

Is that so hard?

Directing Your Life

Besides staying connected, you want to direct your life. These few visualizations will help you do that.

River Of Life and Health Meditation

This one is first and foremost. If you don't do anything else, do this one, as described in the text. It is powerful and cannot possibly hurt anyone, ever.

Blue flame of consciousness

As a part of the River of Life and Health meditation, or alone, envision a blue flame within your forehead, above the eyes. A flame of any kind has been a symbol of consciousness for many years, and a blue flame (as opposed to yellow) burns clean. Let this symbol remind you that there is another part of yourself beyond time and space, benignly observing you living your life, wishing you well, rooting you on. A continual (or even occasional) reminder may serve to keep your ego, with its fears and desires, from blinding you to the fact that you are more than what is obvious.

Body mapping

Again, described in the text. This is how your conscious and subconscious minds can easily and accurately communicate. I don't know a simpler or more effective method.

Visualize and morph

First create an image—a cartoon, perhaps—of the situation as it is; then morph that image into another one that symbolizes the situation as corrected. You can do this any time, either with or without other techniques. You are just communicating with yourself; there are no rules about it that I am aware of.

Awareness hands technique

Imagining your energy body as a duplicate of your physical body, use that body's imagined hands to work on problems of the physical body. If you have a pulled muscle, for example, smooth it out with your awareness hands. Don't worry so much about accuracy, any more than in any other visualization. What you are doing is mobilizing and focusing the forces of the subconscious mind that maintains the body. At least, that's how I think of it. I really don't care so much *why* something works, if it just works.

Resonant energy balloon (rebal)

Also called a circle of white light. You can use this imagined tool for many things. I have "popped a rebal" against mosquitoes and gnats; against poison ivy, against other people's angry or disruptive energy; against temperature that was too hot or too cold to be comfortable. Again, I encourage you to try it on anything you can think of. If it doesn't work, what have you lost? But if it does, you are that much better off.

Control Panel

Last and perhaps most powerful, *create and use your control panel*. What this amounts to is recreating your life to your own design, on an on-going basis. If there's anything more powerful than that, I can't think what it is.

Okay, that's it. We're through. That is, *I* am through, and you are just beginning.

About the Author

Frank DeMarco was co-founder of Hampton Roads Publishing Company, Inc., and for sixteen years was chief editor. He is the author of six previous non-fiction books (*Muddy Tracks, Chasing Smallwood, The Sphere and the Hologram, The Cosmic Internet: Explanations from the Other Side, Afterlife Conversations with Hemingway: A Dialogue on His Life, His Work and the Myth,* and *A Place to Stand*) and two novels (*Messenger: A Sequel to Lost Horizon* and *Babe in the Woods*). He may be reached at *muddytracks@earthlink.net*.

Appendix 1

Excerpt from *The Cosmic Internet*

Space, Time, and the Illusion of Separation

Space produces the illusion of separation, of individuality, of non-belonging, of difference, in a way that would not be possible otherwise. And if space produces the illusion of separation, time produces the effect of delayed consequences. Time, in the way you experience it, sorts out everything just as space does. Last Tuesday is so definitely different from a given date three years ago that you could (and do) stack different people and things in the same space and different time and not have them collide. Time, like space, sorts out the world around you. But they are experienced radically differently: You are not frog-marched through space, inch by inch by inch, always in one direction. But you *are* frog-marched through time. At least, that's how you experience it. But your interpretation of your experience misleads you.

When a moment of time "passes"—that moment does not cease to exist: *You* cease to exist *in it. You* have been carried smoothly to the next moment of time. If you are standing still for five such moments, it looks to you that you moved in time and not in space. But it could equally truly be said that you moved in time-space. That is, moment one exists next to moment two, and you moved from one to two. Then you moved to moment three, then four—and your movement is continuous, predictable and not under your control, so when you get to moment five you assume that the "previous"—which really means previously experienced—moments have somehow ceased to exist.

Your experience tells you that moving through time is like hopping from ice-floe to ice-floe to get across the river, with each previous ice-floe ceasing to exist as soon as you jump from it, and—even more startling, more hazardous—the next ice floe not even coming into existence until you land on it! You never can pause, nor can you do a thing about the situation except to jump in one direction rather than another. If you wanted to rest at any given floe you couldn't, not only because you don't know how to do it, but because what would you do when the floe ceases to exist in the next moment?

What a situation! If it were a true description, you'd be in a pretty bad fix—and, we know, this is how many of you *do* experience your lives. But there's a better way to see it, that will relieve the insecurity. The ice-floe you are standing on does not cease to exist just because you jump from it (or, to put it more closely, are smoothly catapulted from it). And icebergs "to come" are not as-yet-uncreated but already exist, just as they would in a physical-geography metaphor. (Disregard for the moment the fact that you can't see how that could be: Hold the theoretical possibility. All you are doing is creating a space in your mind for a new way of seeing things.)

People who say we have "no time" on "this side" mean by that (though they often do not *know* what they mean) that we are not subject to that unvarying tyranny, moving us along. That is sort of true, in the same way that it is sort of true that we have no space. *Neither statement is true* except in reference to your experience. We have time, we have space—how else could we structure experience? But they are not what they seem to you to be. They are neither prisons nor con-strictions—but they are real limitations. Try to envision a life without limitations and you will end up with fog. *It is the same world.* Canada—the physical Canada—exists "here" as it does "there," because we are not someplace else! The non-physical components of the physical world are—right here! Why would you think they are elsewhere? It isn't even true that you cannot perceive it; it is true only that you cannot perceive it in the same way or using the same faculties that you do the physical world—we might almost say *the rest of* the physical world.

We know that this is a radically different thought for many, so we will try to say it carefully. The non-physical world is right "there" with you, and right "then" with you. How far do you think it is from Baltimore to the non-physical equiva-lent of Baltimore? And why would you think that the physi-cal Baltimore doesn't have its non-physical equivalent? What do you think you build on earth, anyway? But because you misunderstand time, you think that things "pass away" on earth (and presumably in the non-physical earth). Not true in either case.

Where is ancient Rome, say March 1, 250 b.c.? That world on that day is where it always was and always will be. We on this side can "go" there at will; you on your side cannot (normally). And so we on our side we do not get bored, and you on your side get to play with greater consequences. This is the chief difference between our experience of the world and yours. It is a simple concept, but foreign to your usual ways of understanding. We are trying to express it in simple terms devoid of jargon.

Now we are doing quite a bit of hopping ourselves! We are touching on this, touching on that, and not tying up anything. But it is necessary to present several ideas before we can create a model. Continued patience, please.

It is the nature of the physical world—and by "world" we mean not one planet but all of physical creation—to lead its inhabitants to experience one time, one space, then movement to another time, and perhaps to another place. *Spatially* you may move forward, back, right, left, up, down. To Cleveland, to Greenland, to Mars, wherever. The only restrictions on movement are obstacles such as distance, or the nature of the terrain, or whatever. Overcome the obstacle and you may move there. *Temporally*, however, you may move and must move in only one direction—"forward"—and you seemingly cannot vary the speed or direction in which you are carried. In fact, *because* you are carried, it seems to you that you have no control whatever over your movement in time. Now, that is a fair representation, is it not, of your plight on earth? Freedom in three dimensions, no freedom—not even freedom to stop!—in the fourth. Not an incorrect model, but not a very helpful one either. Let us see if we can improve upon it.

We have said that "Canada exists" over here. By that we do not mean that we have a sort of Disneyland version of Canada for people to play pretend in. We mean—Canada here and Canada there are extensions of the same thing, just as you extend "over here" and we "over there." A continuing distortion in these discussions is that spatial and temporal analogies continually sneak in between the lines, because language as it exists reflects your concept of reality. If we were to drop your analogy of this side/that side, we would still need to pick up another, which would have its own defects. That can be a good thing when an analogy has become constricting or very misleading—but until then, why not continue to elaborate on what we're building? It's just a matter of periodic reminders of the limitations of analogy.

Related Titles

If you enjoyed *Imagine Yourself Well,* you may also enjoy
other Rainbow Ridge titles. Read more about them at
www.rainbowridgebooks.com.

The Cosmic Internet: Explanations from the Other Side
by Frank DeMarco

Afterlife Conversations with Hemingway:
A Dialogue on His Life, His Work and the Myth
by Frank DeMarco

Conversations with Jesus: An Intimate Journey
by Alexis Eldridge

Dance of the Electric Hummingbird
by Patricia Walker

Coming Full Circle: Ancient Teachings for a Modern World by
Lynn Andrews

Consciousness: Bridging the Gap Between Conventional Science
and the New Super Science of Quantum Mechanics
by Eva Herr

Jesusgate: A History of Concealment Unraveled
by Ernie Bringas

Messiah's Handbook: Reminders for the Advanced Soul
by Richard Bach

Blue Sky, White Clouds
by Eliezer Sobel

Inner Vegas: Creating Miracles, Abundance, and Health
by Joe Gallenberger

When the Horses Whisper
by Rosalyn Berne

Channeling Harrison, Book 1
by David Young

Lessons in Courage
by Bonnie Glass-Coffin and don Oscar Miro-Quesada

*Dying to Know You: Proof of
God in the Near-Death Experience*
by P.M.H. Atwater

God's Message to the World: You've Got Me All Wrong
by Neale Donald Walsch

Rainbow Ridge Books publishes spiritual, metaphysical, and self-help titles, and is distributed by Square One Publishers in Garden City Park, New York.

To contact authors and editors, peruse our titles, and see submission guidelines, please visit our website at *www.rainbowridgebooks.com.*